CONSUMER BEHAVIOUR

DIPANAKR DUTTA

"Dedicated to my Parents, Friends, and All my respected Teachers"

— Dipankar Dutta

"Education is the proper way to promote compassion and tolerance in society."

— Dalai Lama

Contents

Preface — vii

Acknowledgements — ix

About The Author — xi

1. Consumer Behaviour An Overview — 1

2. Consumer Decision-making Process — 22

3. Models Of Buying Behavior — 34

4. Consumer Involvement And Satisfaction — 45

5. Trends In Consumer Behavior — 60

6. Consumer Protection Act, 2019 — 64

7. Question Bank — 77

Preface

Consumer Behaviour has become vital to survival, in the rapidly changing world of global business. It has assumed tremendous importance for planning marketing strategy and growth in today's competitive scenario.

The book consists of various issues, challenges and opportunities that lie within the periphery of buying behaviour. The very intention of this book is to provide management students with the most current and comprehensive analysis of the field with the help of models and exhibits.

My goal is to provide an analysis of the subject as per the syllabus of BBA. I have tried to lay the necessary basic fundamental concepts of Consumer behaviour, at every stage, and endovenous to show their application in Indian markets. This book contains both theory and insight into Consumer Behaviour for the benefit of students who are curious to know about the buying behaviour of Indian markets.

I expect valuable suggestions for improvements from my dear students and faculty members, which will be helpful for our next edition.

Dipankar Dutta
email- *dipankarpharma1@gmail.com*

Acknowledgements

This book is the end result of the author's own effort, no doubt, but the author completed this task by virtue of the blessings of elders & teachers, the good wishes of well-wishers, and the cooperation of many friends and colleagues. All those who have contributed to this cause of mine definitely deserve thankful acknowledgment. Innumerable persons have contributed to this endeavor and I would like to express my gratitude to all of them who saw me through this book; to all those who provided support, talked things over, read, wrote, offered comments, allowed me to quote their remarks and assisted in the editing, proofreading, and design.

I am thankful to my **Parents**, my best friend **Mr. Saranjit Singha, Prof. Puneet Kumar Garg , Miss. Nimisha Verma, Miss. Aeshwarya Chauhan** for their never-ending cooperation, encouragement, and moral support during the preparation of this book.

I am indebted to the entire team of Notion Press publishers for the effort they have put in for making this book a reality and for helping in the neat execution of the next.

Last but not the least, I beg forgiveness from all those who have been with me over the course of the years and whose names I have failed to mention.

Dipankar Dutta
email- *dipankarpharma1@gmail.com*

About The Author

Over the past few years, Mr. Dipankar Dutta is an educator by profession. Currently associated with JBIT College of Applied Sciences, Dehradun (U.K.), India as an Assistant Professor of Marketing & HR and also pursuing Ph.D. He has pursued Bachelor of Pharmacy, and MBA (Marketing and HR) from Assam University, Silchar (A Central University). He has published many research and review articles in national and international Journals and conferences.

email- *dipankarpharma1@gmail.com*

CHAPTER ONE

Consumer Behaviour An Overview

"<u>*Learning Objective*</u>

- *Explain how a marketer benefits from understanding consumer behavior.*
- *Nature, Scope, Importance of Consumer Behaviour.*
- *Identify those factors that affect a consumer's mindset in consumer decision-making.*
- *Consumer Vs Industrial Buying behavior.*

Lorose

INTRODUCTION

Consumer behavior is comparatively a new field of study which evolved just after the Second World War. The seller's market has disappeared and the buyer's market has come up. So nowadays every marketer tries to understand consumer psychology and in this process, they make every effort to understand how a consumer thinks and behaves in every stage of purchase, finally they try to retain the customer. Marketers expect that by understanding what causes consumers to buy particular goods and services, they will be able to determine—which products are needed in the marketplace, which are obsolete, and how best to present the goods to the consumers.

So consumer behavior is all about understanding the phycology of a consumer and how a consumer selects, buys, and disposes of any particular products and service to satisfy their needs and wants. According to C.L.

Narayana and R.J. Markin, " Consumer behavior is the study of how, why and what people do when they buy products or avail of some services. It attempts to understand the buyer's decision-making process both individually or in groups." According to Engel, Blackwell, and Mansard, 'consumer behavior is the actions and decision processes of people who purchase goods and services for personal consumption.

Nature of Consumer Behaviour

The study of consumer behavior helps in understanding how individuals make decisions to spend their available resources time, money, and efforts while purchasing goods and services. Following are the few point-

1. **Evolving customer preferences**: Change is a natural process. Customers do not buy absolute products or services. Consumer tests and preferences are changing over time depending on the nature of products and trends. For example - earlier people use to buy analog watches but the trend has shifted to digital watches.
2. **Varies from consumer to consumer**: All consumers do not behave in the same manner. Different consumers behave differently. The differences in consumer behavior are due to individual factors such as the nature of the consumers, lifestyle, and culture. For example, some consumers are very much advanced in technology. Some prefer buying all items from online shopping websites while others have trust issues with e-commerce websites. As well as some consumers are very much influenced by the discount factor but some may only select good quality products and services, price is not a constraint for them.
3. **Vary across regions**: Consumer behavior varies across States, regions, and countries. For instance, the behavior of urban consumers is different from that of rural consumers. normally rural consumers are conservative (traditional) in their buying behavior.
4. **Influenced by various factors:** Consumer behavior is influenced by several factors like personal factors, psychological factors, situational factors, social and cultural factors, etc. For example -there are various personal and cultural factors like festival sessions and discount situations when people usually buy, (we will briefly discuss all these factors in the next chapter of this book)

5. **Leads to purchase decision:** Positive consumer behavior leads to a purchase decision. Customers may buy a particular product or service depending on various buying motives.

Scope of Consumer Behaviour

The scope of consumer behavior is vast. Because the consumer is the king of business. Marketers must try to understand consumer behavior so that they can offer consumers greater satisfaction. The scope of consumer behavior is as follows-

1. **Demand Forecasting:** Consumer behavior helps in demand forecasting. Forecasting helps them to find out the unfulfilled demands in the market easily. If the company knows what their consumer wants, it can design and produce the product accordingly. The behavior of the consumer plays an important role in forecasting the demand for the products. In addition, it helps the company to identify the market opportunity available to them.
2. **Helps to improve marketing strategy:** The study of consumers helps a firm or organization to improve its marketing strategy. If marketers know the phycology of consumers then they set their marketing strategy according to the marketers. For example - Children's toys and chocolate are mostly advertised on cartoon channels because companies can easily educate their target customers.
3. **Selecting Target Market:** Consumer behavior helps the organization select its target group from the market. Studying and identifying consumer behavior helps them to know the consumer segments with distinct features and wants. It helps in segmenting the overall market into different groups.
4. **Market Mix:** Proper development and designing of all-important elements like product, price, place, and promotion are essential for every business. It helps them to identify the likes and dislikes of the customers. This allows marketers to design optimum marketing mix plans and improve the effectiveness of marketing strategies. The proper implementation of a marketing mix helps organizations to attract more customers, thereby increasing profit.

5. **Product positioning:** Product Positioning is a marketing technique intended to present products in the best possible way to different target audiences. Positioning is the process of distinguishing a brand from its competitors so that it becomes the preferred brand in defined segments of the market. Effective Product Positioning requires a clear understanding of customer behavior & needs.

6. **Consumer behavior and social marketing**: Social marketing is the application of marketing strategies and tactics to alter or create behaviors that have a positive effect on the targeted individual or society as a whole. As true for commercial marketing strategy, a successful social marketing strategy requires a sound understanding of consumer behavior. If an organization is able to determine what satisfies consumers, the organization can implement the marketing concept and better predict how consumers will respond to different marketing programs. Social marketing has the primary goal of achieving the "common good". Traditional commercial marketing aims are primarily financial, though they can have positive social effects as well. In the context of public health, social marketing would promote general health, raise awareness and induce changes in behavior. Social marketing is one of the modern marketing concepts that have become a tool for achieving success in companies, and through this research, we aim to highlight the role that social marketing plays in influencing customer behavior.

Factors influencing Consumer Behavior

There are various factors that may affect consumer behavior. Exhibit 1.1 represent a general model of consumer behavior that describes various factors influencing consumer behavior.

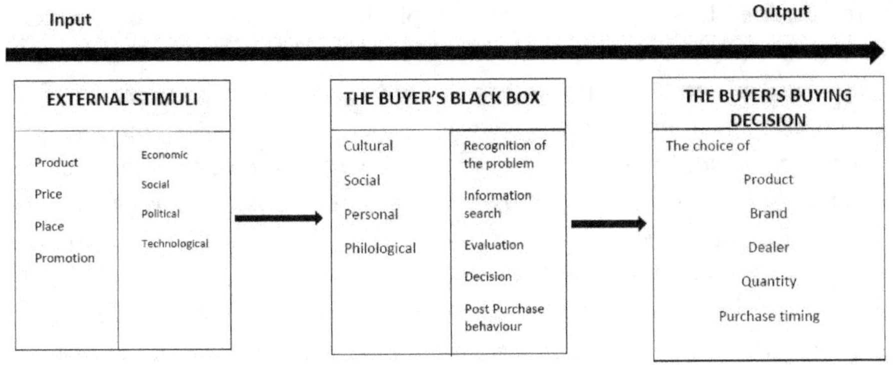

Exhibit 1.1: General model of Consumer behavior

The buying process mainly starts by analyzing external stimuli. External stimuli are divided into Marketing stimuli and Environmental Stimuli. Marketing stimuli are nothing but the 4 Ps of marketing i.e. Product, price, place, and promotions. These are the most important aspect of marketing. A company can formulate and change these 4 Ps in such a manner as to capture a large share of the market. Each element of the marketing mix has the potential to affect the buying process at various stages.

- Product: The uniqueness of the product, the physical appearance, and the packaging can influence buying decision of a consumer.
- Pricing: Pricing strategy does affect the buying behavior of consumers. Marketers must consider the price sensitivity of the target customers while fixing prices.
- Promotion: The various elements of promotion such as advertising, publicity, public relations, personal selling, and sales promotion affect the buying behavior of consumers. Marketers select the promotion mix after considering the nature of customers.
- Place: The channels of distribution and the place of distribution affect the buying behavior of consumers. Marketers make an attempt to select the right channel and distribute the products in the right place.

Environmental stimuli consist of economic, technological, political, and cultural aspects. These factors are also very much responsible for buying behavior of customers. But as these are external factors that vary from person to person so marketer does not have any control over environmental factors. The buyer's black box typically consists of the buyer's characteristics and the buyer's decision-making process. The buyer's characteristics are again divided into cultural, social, personal, and psychological characteristics. These aspects are internal to each person and differ from person to person that's why it is very difficult for a marketer to influence them. The other part is the consumer decision-making process. This starts from recognizing the problem, in this phase, a consumer is facing a difference between his or her desired state and the actual state and identifying the need. Then the consumer goes for information search and evaluation of alternatives. The most important part of this process is the final buying decision. Here the consumer has to decide which products satisfy his or her needs in the best way. Marketers try to study the external stimuli and consumers' black boxes in order to expand their market share.

Microfactors influencing Consumer Behavior

Along with the above factors, there are also four microfactors that influence consumer behavior. These are mentioned in Exhibit 1.2 and discussed in the following section.

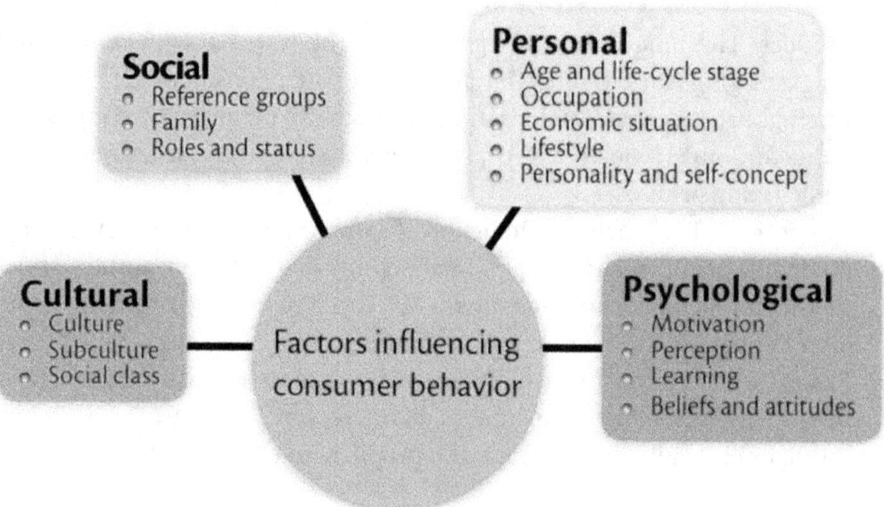

Exhibit 1.2 : Microfactors influencing Consumer behavior

These factors cause consumers to develop product and brand preferences. These factors impact whether or not your target customer buys your product. Cultural factors play an important role in affecting consumer buying behavior.

Cultural Factor: Cultural factors are one of the major factors which affect buying behavior in a large geographical area. Culture is the set of basic values, perceptions, wants, and behaviors learned by a member of society from a family or place of residence. Culture is the most basic cause of a person's wants and behavior. We can also define culture as the learned values, perceptions, wants, and behavior from family and other important institutions.

For example - India is a culturally diversified country. Culture and religious festivals have a huge impact on Indian buying patterns. Usually, people buy in festival sessions. Various companies and shopping malls give huge discounts on these occasions like consumer durables products, textiles, leaders goods, and so on. Obviously, Companies and marketers take advantage of these festivals and come out with new marketing strategies and try to push their goods and services through intense promotions schemes like - buy one get one free, gift coupons, discounts, exchange offers, etc. to inhibit consumer buying moods. Cultural factors are very much responsible for buying behavior of any consumer. The behavioral patterns are developed from the culture where he or she has been brought up. For example - Indian consumers are very much habituated to ayurvedic products because our cultural beliefs are ideologies are very much inclined towards Ayurveda. While in western countries brides wear white dresses at their wedding, Indian women normally wear a white dress or white saree only when someone dies or when she becomes a widow.

Subculture: Subcultures are groups of people within a culture with shared value systems based on everyday life experiences and situations. It provides more specific identification and socialization for members belonging to a particular geographical location, racial group, or religion.

Social classes: Social classesare society's relatively permanent and ordered divisions whose members share similar values, interests, and behaviors. Measured by a combination of occupation, income, education, wealth, and other variables. The major social classes are - Upper class, Middle class, Working class, and Lower class. Obviously, the buying patterns and brand selection are different in these social classes. For example- An upper-class gentlemen want to travel by business class ticket on an airplane but a middle-class person will prefer an economy class ticket.

Social Factor: Social factors that influence consumer purchasing include family, peers, roles, and status. Family members such as a spouse, children, and parents can exert a strong influence on the consumer's purchasing behavior. Peer pressure is also a strong factor that determines a consumer's purchasing choices. Everyone belongs to a group of some sort, from friends to neighbors and coworkers. A consumer's behavior is also influenced by social factors, such as the consumer's reference group, family, social roles, and social status.

Reference groups: Every individual has some people around who influence him/her in any way. Reference groups comprise people that whom individuals compare themselves. Every individual knows some people in society who become their idols in due course of time. A reference group is a group that an individual uses as a base while forming his/her values and manners and is very important with regard to consumer behaviors. They give information to their group members about special products and brands and provide individuals with the opportunity of comparing the manners and attitudes of the group with their own thoughts. They affect individuals in accordance with the norms of the group. Reference groups especially determine the desired and undesired products. Moreover, they are inclined to affect the choice of products, information process, form of manner, and shopping behaviors of consumers. Marketing managers feel a need for defining reference groups along with consumers in the target markets that they have determined. Because reference groups have the power of affecting the lifestyles, manners, and self-expressions of consumers. Reference groups are divided into primary as well as secondary groups. **Primary groups** consist of family members, friends, neighbors, and colleagues. **Secondary groups** consist of those groups which are more formal in nature and people have less interaction with them like professional groups, religious groups, trade union groups, etc. Reference groups usually have **opinion leaders**. An opinion leader is a person who has mastered a certain market or industry and gained the community's trust. An insider or decision-maker in that market or industry is considered an opinion leader. They have a readership or fan base who see them as a reliable source of information on their hobbies. Because of their power to shape the market and consumer trends, opinion leaders are crucial. They frequently hold the power in the market to be the first to utilize a new good or service, and they have the ability to influence others by sharing their knowledge and opinions, which may have an effect on how their audience uses the good or service. Reference groups are generally two types- primary and secondary reference groups. Primary reference groups consist of people one interacts with on a regular basis like - friends, family members, co-workers, etc. Secondary groups share an indirect relationship with the consumer. These groups are more formal and individuals do not interact with them on a regular basis, for Example - Religious Associations, Political Parties, Clubs, etc.

Family: Family plays an important role in buying behavior of each and every person. Family members constitute the most influential primary reference in a buyer's life. Especially Indian consumers have a high degree of family orientation because family bonds are stronger bonds than any other group. Each family members influences and gets influenced by a family member depending upon his role, life cycle stage, and relationship dynamics plays

For example, during any festival, people use to buy clothes for their family. Family preferences about a particular brand or item play a significant role during a family marriage.

Roles and Status: A person is influenced by the role that he holds in society. A social role is a set of attitudes and activities that an individual is supposed to have and do according to his profession and his position at work, his position in the family, his gender, etc., and the expectation of the people around him. Suppose a person is in a high position, his buying behavior will be influenced largely by his status. For example- A person who is a Chief Executive Officer in a company will buy according to his status while staff or an employee of the same company will have different buying patterns.

Personal Factors: Personal Factors play an important role in affecting consumer buying behavior. Personal factors generally comprise the following-

1. Age and life cycle stage,
2. Occupation and economic conditions,
3. Personality and Self-concept,
4. Lifestyle and status.

Age and life cycle stage: A consumer does not buy the same products or services in 20 or 70 years. His lifestyle, values, hobbies, and environment evolve throughout his life. For example - during his life, a person may change his diet from unhealthy foods like - junk food, cold drinks, and alcohol to a purely healthy diet. Similarly the stage in the life cycle also greatly influences a consumer's consumption patterns. Phycological life cycle stages also matter. So usually marketers try to generate new needs depending upon critical life events of consumers like - marriage, birthday, relocation, career change, etc.

Occupation, economic condition, and Lifestyle: The occupation of an individual plays a significant role in influencing a consumer's buying decision. An individual's nature of his job has a direct influence on the products and brands he or picks for himself/herself. For example - A banker or doctor will buy more formal shirts rather than casual ones. An individual's designation and the nature of work influence his buying decisions. Generally a low-level worker purchases business suits, and ties for himself. An individual working on the shop floor can't afford to wear premium brands daily to work. Likewise, College goers and students would prefer casuals as compared to professionals who would be more interested in buying formal shirts and trousers.

Along with occupation economic conditions also influences consumption patterns and product choice. Persons, disposable income plays a significant role in buying behavior. Disposable income is the amount of money that an individual or household has to spend or save after income taxes have been deducted. At the macro level, disposable personal income is a key economic indicator that can determine buying behavior of any individual.

Another important factor is a person's lifestyle. The lifestyle of a person involves his consumption pattern, his behavior in the marketplace, practices, habits, conventional ways of doing things, allocation of income, and reasoned actions. It reflects an individual's attitudes, values, interests, and views toward society. A person's pattern of living is expressed in his/her psychographics. It involves measuring consumer activities such as the nature of work, hobbies, shopping, sports events, etc.

Personality and Self-concept: Personality is the composite sum of an individual's psychological traits, characteristics, motives, habits, attitudes, beliefs, and outlooks. In other words, personality is nothing but the psychological characteristics that both determine and reflect how a person responds to his or her environment. Although personality tends to be consistent and enduring, it may change abruptly in response to major life events, as well as gradually over time. Three theories of personality are prominent in the study of consumer behavior: Neo-Freudian theory, psychoanalytic theory, and trait theory.

Neo-Freudian Theory

Freud believed that personality was Biological and rooted in genetics and groomed as a result of early childhood experiences. This group of researchers who laid emphasis on the process of socialization came to be known as the Neo. To form a personality, social relationships are very important.

Based on this, consumers are classified into three personality types –

- Complaint Personalities – They prefer love and affection and so they move towards them and so they prefer known brands.
- Aggressive Personalities – They tend to move against others and they show off their need for power, success, etc. which is quite manipulative.
- Detached Personalities – They are not much aware of brands and are more self-reliant and independent.

Marketers also tend to use Neo-Freudian theories while segmenting markets and positioning their products

The Psychoanalytic Theory of Freud

Sigmund Freud, the father of psychology, became famous with his psychoanalytic theory of personality. Freud believed that there are three forces that work in an individual's psychology. They are id; superego; and ego. He thought that an individual's personality is determined by the interaction of the id, ego, and superego.

Id: includes the instincts and is present at birth, which pushes an individual toward the immediate gratification of his needs. Id stresses on immediate fulfillment of needs. Id is the personality component made up of unconscious psychic energy which satisfies basic urges, needs, and desires.

Superego: On the other hand, inhibits the impulses of the id, and influences the individual toward conforming to all of the moral principles. It is the aspect of personality that holds all our moral standards and ideals that we acquire from both our parents and society.

Ego: Mediates between the impulses of the id and the inhibitors of the superego and shows the individual ways of satisfying his needs in socially acceptable ways thus creating balance in the individual.

He also believed that individuals pass through a number of sequential stages from his birth to the first few years of life. One's personality develops on the basis of the amount of frustration and anxiety he faces at each of these stages.

<u>**Trait Theory**</u>

Traits are the features of an individual or tendencies of an individual in a particular manner. Traits help in defining the behavior of consumers. According to Trait theorists, an individual's personality makeup stems from the traits that he possesses, and the identification of traits is important. The few most common traits are- Outgoing, Sad, Stable, Serious, Relaxed, Self-assured, Practical, And Imaginative.

Trait theory is representative of multi-personality theories. Trait theory is based on certain assumptions, such as traits that are certainly stable in nature and a limited number of traits that are common to most people.

According to Trait theorists, an individual's personality makeup stems from the traits that he possesses, and the identification of traits is essential. The trait theories can be of two broad categories, viz., Simple trait theories and general trait theories.

Self Concept is also a very important factor that affects consumer behavior. Morris Rosenberg defines Self Concept as – "The totality of individual thoughts and feelings having reference to himself as an object". In general, consumers use products to support their self-concepts. Products and brands are important ways consumers reflect and shape their identities. Self-concept also relates to how consumers want others to see them. Self-concept is a self-image or identity made up of a subjective collection of thoughts, perceptions, and feelings. It includes personality, abilities, occupation, and the various personal and professional roles the consumer takes on.

Self-concepts fall into two categories:

- **Actual self** – How the consumer actually is. This is less subjective than the other types of self-concept and includes facts like occupation, age, gender, income, etc. usually consumer buy and use products and services which suit their occupation, age, and gender. Marketers try to fulfill their Actual self to satisfy consumers.

- **Ideal self**– The consumer's perception of who she would ideally like to be. Prospects measure their actual self against their ideal self. They want to achieve their ideal self. The gap between the actual and ideal self can create a strong motivation to buy products to bring the actual self closer to the ideal self.

Self-concepts of the actual and ideal selves also fall into two further categories:

Private self: Who the consumer is or wants to be for him/ herself (for example: adventurous, friendly, happy), rather than how he or she wants others to see them. Marketing messages can appeal to the private self with internal benefits like happiness, health, and spirituality.

Public self: How the consumer thinks other people see him, and how he wants to be seen (for example: intelligent, attractive, and successful). An organization's marketing can appeal to how prospects want others to see them by portraying the benefits they want to achieve and showing other people's reactions.

Market research survey helps an organization uncover hidden self-concepts. This will allow any organization to position their company and products to support consumers' self-concepts so they connect with their product emotionally and develop loyalty.

Here are some ways that self-concepts affect buying:

- **Every market has different self-concepts:** Marketers must go for market research to find out their poisoning of products according to the buyers self- concept.
- **Self-concept is a work in progress:** Self-concepts are always developing and consumers are always striving to achieve them. The drive to support self-concept is always active.
- **Support, rather than change, self-concept:** People tend to oppose change to their self-concept, and a conflict or inconsistency with self-concept can be seen as threatening. The more important a belief is to a prospect's self-concept, the more he will resist changing it. So a marketer must try to position their product so that it can able to support self-concept, rather than try to change it.

- **Self-concept defends self-esteem:** When a product supports a consumer's self-concept, she feels understood and validated, and that she has gained some control over her emotions by buying the product.

Phycological factor: Finally at the individual level various psychological factors like- motivation, perception, learning, belief, and attitude affect the buying behavior of consumers.

Motivation: Motivation is the process that initiates, guides, and maintains goal-oriented behavior. Motivation is the internal feeling that makes a person buy a particular product or service in order to satisfy a necessity. Once a need is aroused, a condition of tension emerges that leads the consumer to minimize or remove the tension. Marketers try to create products and services that will provide the desired benefits and permit the consumer to reduce this tension.

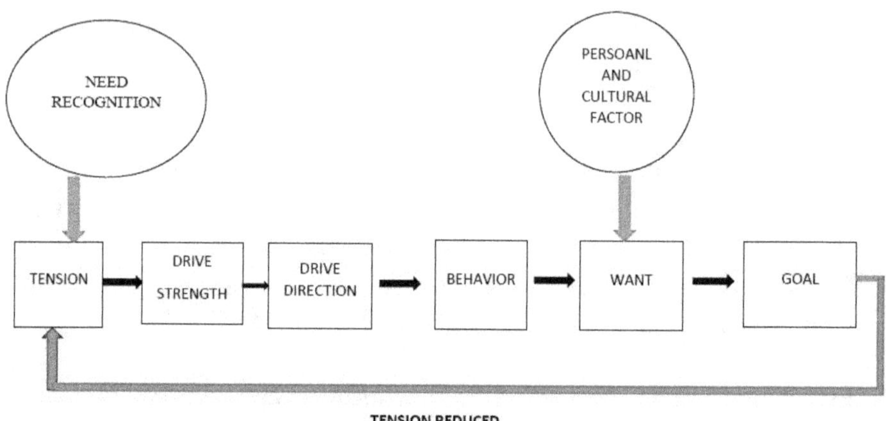

Exhibit 1.3: Overview of the motivation process

Actually, a person's motivation develops into a significant defining feature that affects their purchasing habit. Maslow's theory of the hierarchy of needs, which he developed, is a well-known theory of motivation. It lays the groundwork for five different levels of human needs, starting with psychological needs and progressing through safety needs, social needs, esteem needs, and finally self-actualization needs. Our fundamental needs and security demands are often prioritized above all others among these criteria. For example, a person would fulfill his most basic needs first like food, shelter, cloth, etc. and it would possibly be advanced to meet some higher needs.

Perception: Perception is the process by which people select, organize, and interpret information to form a meaningful picture of the world from three perceptual processes: Selective attention, Selective distortion, and Selective retention. Perception depends on the experience that people have had with the product and also on any prior knowledge about a product that they may have gained from others. Selective attention is the tendency for people to screen out most of the information to which they are exposed. Selective distortion is the tendency for people to interpret information in a way that will support what they already believe. Selective retention is the tendency to remember good points made about a brand they favor and to forget good points about competing brands.

As a consumer, perception becomes shaped by advertising, word of mouth, past experiences, social media, pricing, quality, and customer service. Consumers make choices based on price, need opportunity, packaging, brand ethics, and more. Shifting how consumers perceive these things can dramatically impact whether they purchase any given brand and why. If consumers perceive that a product or a brand is a bad choice, whether it's based on ethos, quality, or price, then it really doesn't matter if it actually is a bad choice because customer perception dictates consumer action, and that action becomes reality. If marketers can create a public perception that their product is high quality, their prices are fair, their service is responsible and attentive and that the brand stands behind what they do, they'll gain more customers and enjoy great loyalty.

Learning: Learning is the changes in an individual's behavior arising from experience. Elements of consumer learning are- Drives or motives, Stimuli, Cues, Responses, and Reinforcement. According to Kotler's Definition, learning involves changes in an individual's behavior arising out of his / her experience. Most human behavior is learned over time, out of the experience.

Basically, consumer learning is a process that evolves and changes as consumers acquire knowledge from experience, observation, and interactions with others. This newly acquired knowledge affects future behavior.

Consumer Behavioral Learning Theories

There are various theories that are developed to explain learning. Below are the major theories related to consumer behavior.

Classical conditioning Theory: Ivan Pavlov, a famous Russian physiologist, developed the concept of classical conditioning. This theory refers to learning through repetition. It is such a kind of behavioral theory that says, when a stimulus is connected to or paired with another stimulus, it serves to produce the same response even when used alone. For example- if you usually listen to the news at 9 PM and have dinner too at 9 PM while watching the news then eventually the sound of the news at 9 PM may make you hungry even though you are not actually hungry or even if dinner is not ready.

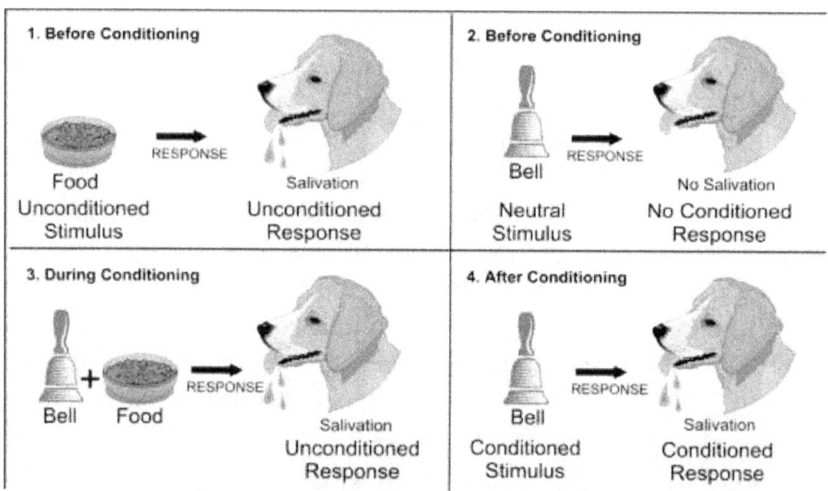

Exhibit 1.3:Pavlov Experiment on Classical Conditioning

Ivan Pavlov conducted extensive tests on dogs to examine how different stimuli—such as bells, different colors, or lights—are accompanied by conditioned reactions in the dogs, such as salivation. In his experiment, he used a dog that was kept in a room and regularly exposed to the sound of the bell as a stimulus. A piece of food (usually meat) was then presented, which caused the dog to salivate. Food and the bell were introduced in order over a period of time (about seven days), with the bell appearing at each trial. a point at which the bell's ringing would normally cause salivation even in the absence of food. According to neurological theory, the stimulus.

Implications of Classical conditioning in Consumer behavior

1) Message repetition: Repetition occurs when customers hear a brand's name and marketing message again. It strengthens the link between the conditioned and unconditioned stimuli. It increases brand awareness and hence also increases sales. For example- Myntra and Flipkart advertisements are very much repetitively shown on YoutTube which creates brand awareness As a result, it slowed the pace of forgetting.

2)Stimulus generalization: Responding the same way to slightly different stimuli is called stimulus generalization. Here consumers confuse them with the original products they have been advertised. For example- What comes to mind when you see the Tide laundry detergent symbol? The most likely answer is the color orange, clean clothes, and distinctive containers sold in supermarkets. So although most consumers associate Tide with washing clothes powder they respond in a similar way to tide laundry service as well because of stimulus generalization.

3) Stimulus discrimination: Stimulus discrimination means the selection of a specific stimulus from among similar stimuli. Here the main objective of marketers is to position the brand in a unique way that would help it to differentiate amongst similar product categories. Apple is a prominent example of differentiating a product.

Operant Conditioning Theory: Consumer learning is based ontrial and error. Consumers learn through a process of trial and error in which certain purchasing behaviors provide better results (rewards) than other purchasing behaviors. A positive experience is essential in instructing the person to repeat a particular behavior.

Positive Reinforcement: Positive outcomes that strengthen the likelihood of a specific response.

Example: Ad showing beautiful hair as a reinforcement to buy shampoo.

Negative Reinforcement: Unpleasant or negative outcomes that serve to encourage a specific behavior.

Example: Ad showing wrinkled skin as reinforcement to buy skin cream.

Beliefs and attitudes: Marketers can use beliefs and attitudes for customizing their products according to the need of the customer because beliefs and attitudes play a major role in the buying behavior of a customer. An attitude is a pre-acquired inclination to favor or disfavor a person, place, situation, or product. The consumer's attitude is the outcome of examining specific aspects in their mind, and attitude, or the "black box," is what shapes the consumer's perception of the product as excellent or poor. Consumer attitudes are made up of three basic elements: beliefs, sentiments, and behavioral intentions toward a particular good or service. These three elements are taken into account when a firm launches a marketing campaign that promotes a brand or any commercial establishment. These three elements work together to form the essential framework and reflect elements that influence how consumers react to products. Consumer beliefs may be further divided into three categories: positive beliefs, negative beliefs, and beliefs that fall into the neutral category since they are neither positive nor bad. These beliefs can be a consequence of their personal experience or because of their interaction with other people.

Organizational Buying behavior

Organizational Buying Behaviour or Industrial buying behavior is a complex decision-making and communication process involving the selection and procurement of products and services by organizational buyers. Or Organizational buying is the decision-making process by which formal organizations establish the need for purchased products and services and identify, evaluate and choose among the available alternative brands and suppliers. In simple words, Organizational behavior refers to the buying behavior of organizations that buy products for business use, resell, or to make other products.

Characteristics of organizational buying behavior: Buying behavior varies greatly between consumers and businesses.Each organization has its own business philosophy that guides its buying behavior. Following are the basic five characteristics of organizational buying behavior-

1. The number of participants: Organizational buying generally involves multiple persons like influencers who identify the need for the product, the final user of the product, the organization's financial conditions, gatekeepers who screen potential suppliers, and senior management who approved the funds for the particular purchase. But consumer buying usually involves one or two participants, including the final user of the products.

2. Influencing factors and motivators: The influences on consumer buying behavior usually consist of basic needs, friends, family, occupation, etc. But various environmental cum organizational factors such as competitive pressure, technological advancement, and changing macroeconomic factors are the major influencing factors of organizational buying behavior.

3. Organizational buying decisions frequently involve a range of complex technical dimensions. For example, A purchasing agent for a pharmaceutical company must consider a number of technical factors before ordering such as product quality, transport cost, storage

requirement, etc.

4. Timing complexity: The period between the marketer's initial contact with the consumer and the purchase decision is usually rather long due to the corporate decision-making process. Because numerous new elements might enter the picture during this lag period, the marketer's ability to monitor and react to these changes is important.

5. A precise categorization of organizations is impossible. Each company has its own personality and method of operation which guides its buying behavior.

Organizational Buying situation:

Organizational buying is also known as institutional buying or business-to-business (B2B) buying. The process begins when an organization discovers a demand for commodities. Then they collect information to compare and contrast competing brands' products and services. Finally, they make a final purchase decision. The organizational buying situation can be divided into four types i.e. Straight rebuy, Modified rebuy, systems buy, and New task buy.

- Straight rebuy: In this buying situation, only purchasing department is involved. Purchasing department gets information from the inventory control department or section to reorder the material and they seek quotations from vendors from an approved list.
- Modified rebuy: In this buying situation, there is a modification to the specification of the product or specification related to delivery. Executives apart from the purchasing department are generally involved in the buying decisions. In a modified rebuy situation company usually looks for an additional supplier or modifies the approved vendor list based on the specification.
- System buys: System buying is a process in which an organization gives full order of a new system to a single organization. The buying organization knows that no single party is producing all the units in the system. But it wants the system seller to engineer the system, produce the units from various vendors, and assemble, fabricate or construct the system.
- New task buys: In this situation, the buyer is buying the product for the first time. As the cost of the product and consumption value becomes higher more numbers of executives are involved in the buying process.

Stages in Organizational buying

Consumer buying stages (Briefly discussed in Chapter number 2) and organizational buying stages are different. Exhibit 1.4 explain the stages of organizational buying stages.

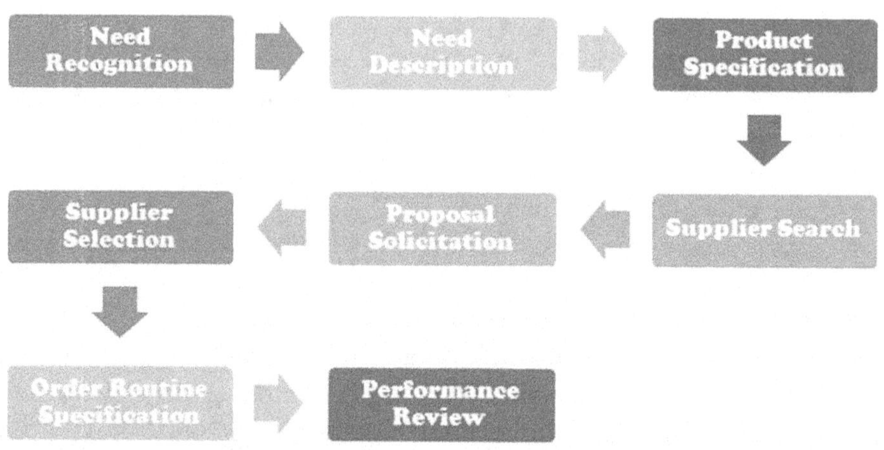

Exhibit 1.4: Stages in Organizational buying

Need recognition: In this stage, the organization recognizes a problem or need that can be met by acquiring a good or service. During this stage, someone in the company recognizes the need that can be met by acquiring a good or service.

Need description: In this stage, the buyer company describes the general characteristic and quantity of a needed item.

Product specification: At this stage of the business buying process buying organization decides the technical specifications of the product to be purchased.

Supplier search: At this stage of the business buying process buying organization tries to find out the best vendors. At this phase, the buyer identifies the most suitable supplier through trade directories and then contacts other companies, trade advertisements, trade shows, and through the internet.

Proposal solicitation: At this stage, the buyer invites qualified suppliers to submit proposals.

Supplier section: This is the stage of the business buying process in which the buyer reviews the proposal which was submitted by the seller and selects a supplier or suppliers.

Order routine specification: At this stage of the business buying process buying organization negotiates the final order with the supplier, listing the technical specifications, quantity needed, expected time of delivery, return policies, warranties, etc.

Performance review: This is the last stage of the business buying process during this stage the buyer periodically reviews the performance of the chosen supplier.

CHAPTER TWO

Consumer Decision-Making Process

Learning Objective

- *Consumer decision-making process.*
- *Pre and Post buying behavior*
- *Diffusion of innovation*

Consumer decision-making process:

Understanding consumer behavior is very much essential to know how a consumer makes a purchase decision and how the consumer will use or dispose of a particular product. The consumer decision-making process involves five basic steps. This is the process by which consumers evaluate making a purchasing decision. The 5 steps are problem recognition, information search, alternatives evaluation, purchase decision, and post-purchase evaluation.

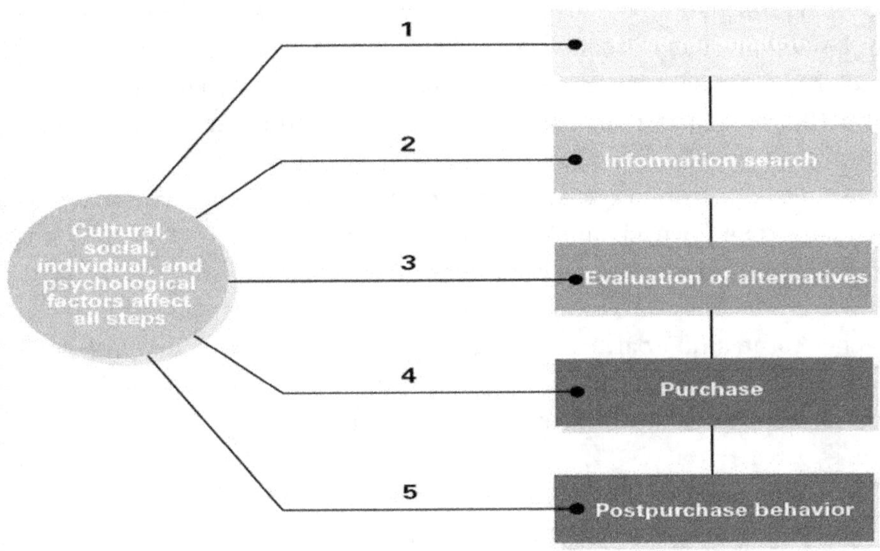

Exhibit 2.1: Consumer decision-making process

Along with these 5 stages, a physiological process is also associated with the decision-making process i.e. Motivation, perception, Attitude formation, Integration, and Learning.

Need Recognition:

The first step of the consumer decision-making process is recognizing the need for a service or product. This is the first and most important stage of the buying process because every sale begins when a customer becomes aware that they have a need for a product or service. When a consumer feels the imbalance between his desired state and actual state the need is recognized by him. There are various internal as well as external stimuli responsible for need generation. Internal Stimuli: In this, the need generation occurs due to internal drives like Thrust, Hunger, sight, smell, touch, etc. External stimuli: Need that generates in response to any Advertisement, Radio Jingle, Pamphlets, etc. Any type of financial change, changes in employment status, lifestyle, and knowledge may prompt anyone to develop new needs and wants.

Information Search:

After identifying the need, the consumers start collecting valuable information about how they can meet their needs. For research, the consumer uses both Internal and External sources. Consumers usually do internal information searches by recalling information in their own memory for low-involvement products. External information search is also classified into two types- Marketing controlled and non-marketing-controlled. Sometimes consumers can able to search only those items that are highly controlled by the marketing team of any company. And sometimes consumers try to find out various information about products or services by using their own channels. Information can also be obtained through recommendations from people having previous experiences with products. At this level, consumers tend to consider risk management and prepare a list of the features of a particular brand. This is done so because most people do not want to regret their buying decision. Information for products and services can be obtained through several sources:

- Personal Sources: The needs are discussed with family and friends who provided product recommendations. The consumer also searches for information using the internet. If the consumer acquires enough information, then he may make a purchase decision immediately. However, if he fails to gather sufficient information, he may wait or suppress the need. Or repeat the procedure until he finds the valuable information.
- Public sources: Radio, newspapers,s and magazines.
- Commercial sources: Advertisements, promotional campaigns, salespeople, or packaging of a particular product.
- Experiential sources: The own experience of a customer of using a particular brand.

Evaluation of Alternatives:
The next step in the forgoing process is the evaluation of the alternatives. Here, the consumer has to choose between the researched Brands, Products, and Services. Once it has been determined by the customer what can satisfy their need, they will start seeking out the best option available. This evaluation can be based upon different factors like quality, price, or any other factor which are important for customers. They may compare prices or read reviews and then select a product that satisfies their parameters the most. Marketers must consider the parameters & features based on which consumers evaluate the products. They must inculcate these features into their products while manufacturing. Also, promote these

features while marketing their products.

Appropriate alternatives: The awareness set is composed of three subcategories of considerable importance to marketers. i.e. evoked set, inept set, inert set.

- Evoked set: The evoked set or consideration set contains brands or products one will evaluate. For evoke set customer will analyze product attributes, use cutoff criteria, and Rank attribute by importance.
- Inept set: The inept set consists of brands found to be completely unworthy of further consideration.
- Inert set: The inert set contains brands of which the consumer is aware but basically indifferent.

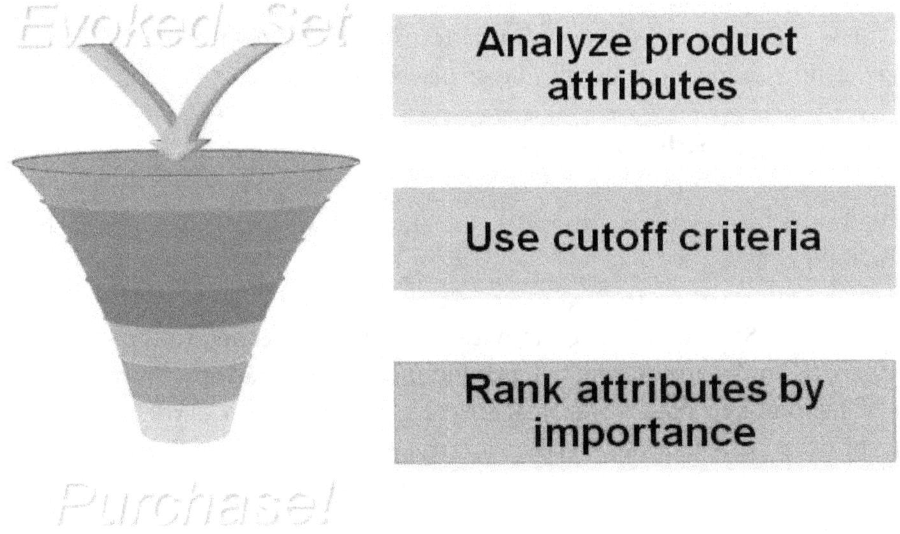

Exhibit 2.2: Decision-making process for evoked set

Purchase Decision:

After a detailed evaluation of the alternatives, the consumer makes the purchase decision. He will choose and buy the most suitable option that perfectly satisfies his need. At this stage, the consumer has evaluated all facts and has arrived at a logical conclusion which is either based upon the influence of marketing campaigns or upon emotional connections or personal experiences, or a combination of both. In this stage, marketers must work on their selling skills and sales pitch. Their pitch must be effective and capable of closing the deal instantly.

Pre-Purchase Behavior

When a consumer realizes the needs, he goes for an information search. He does the same so that he can make the right decision. He gathers information about the following –

- Product Brands
- Products Variations
- Product Quality
- Product Alternatives.

The consumer can gather information about a product depending on his age, gender, education, and product's price, risk, and acceptance.

Types of Search Activities

The information search activity can be classified into various types such as the following –

- Specific: Specific kinds of activities are directly related to the problem. These kinds of requirements need immediate assistance.
- Ongoing: Consumers go on with their research for a particular period of time if they decide if they want to buy a particular product. Ongoing activities basically show the work in progress.
- Incidental: Now, anything that we observe incidentally or just accidentally or naturally comes under incidental research. Such information can be observed in our daily routine lives.

The following are the information sources available –
The information sources are of two types which are listed under

- **Internal Sources** – Internal sources include the consumer himself. Here he himself recalls the information that is stored in his memory and uses his experiences.

- **External Sources** – External sources of information include all sorts of interpersonal communication with the external environment such as friends, family, marketing people, advertisements, etc.

Pre-Purchase Behavior

When a consumer realizes the needs, he goes for an information search. He does the same so that he can make the right decision. He gathers information about the following –

- Product Brands
- Products Variations
- Product Quality
- Product Alternatives.

The consumer can gather information about a product depending on his age, gender, education, and product's price, risk, and acceptance.

Types of Search Activities: The information search activity can be classified into various types such as the following –

- **Specific**: Specific kinds of activities are directly related to the problem. These kinds of requirements need immediate assistance.
- **Ongoing**: Consumers go on with their research for a particular period of time if they decide if they want to buy a particular product. Ongoing activities basically show the work in progress.
- **Incidental**: Now, anything that we observe incidentally or just accidentally or naturally comes under incidental research. Such information can be observed in our daily routine lives.

The following are the information sources available –
The information sources are of two types which are listed under

- **Internal Sources** – Internal sources include the consumer himself. Here he himself recalls the information that is stored in his memory and uses his experiences.
- **External Sources** – External sources of information include all sorts of interpersonal communication with the external environment such as

friends, family, marketing people, advertisements, etc.

Post-Purchase Behavior:

The purchase of the product is followed by a post-purchase evaluation which refers to analyzing whether the product was helpful for the consumer or not. If the product has matched the expectations of the customer, they will serve as a brand ambassador who can influence other potential consumers which will increase the customer base of that particular brand. The same is true for negative experiences; however, they can halt the journey of potential customers toward the product. It is the last but most essential stage of the process. In this, the post-purchase behavior of the consumer is analyzed. It gives feedback to the marketer about the Success and Failure of the product. Marketers focus on this stage because it has the potential to evoke subsequent sales. They can also get their products marketed by a powerful tool, i.e., Word-of-Mouth.

Cognitive Dissonance

Cognitive dissonance is a post-purchase behavior. It is a psychological phenomenon that refers to the discomfort felt at a discrepancy between what you already know or believe, and new information or interpretation. Leon Festinger first investigated cognitive dissonance. Cognitive dissonance refers to a situation involving conflicting attitudes, beliefs,s or behavior. In simple terms, it is "inconsistency". Examples- Someone who smokes knows that smoking is injurious to health. This produces a feeling of mental discomfort.

Example of cognitive dissonance - A customer's reaction after he was involved in the process of purchasing some high-involvement item, usually a very expensive one creates doubt and anxiety in the mind of the customer, especially when the degree of commitment is high. This dissonance often leads to consumption guilt- which is a negative emotion or feelings aroused by the usage of expensive products.

Why Cognitive Dissonance is important for Marketers?

The concept "cognitive dissonance" is of great significance in consumer behavior and marketers have a lot of interest in analyzing the post-purchase behavior of consumers, more particularly about the dissonance experienced by them. After selling a product, the marketers may not have direct contact with the customers. The post-purchase behavior of a customer has been influenced by a number of social factors in which the marketer may not get any direct role. As far as durable and highly involved goods are concerned, before deciding whether the customer is satisfied /dissatisfied, they have to encounter a stage termed as Cognitive Dissonance. It is important to not only acquire new consumers but also retain the existing ones by satisfying their expectations and providing value as a positive brand image, which is a crucial role for marketers. In order to implement a successful strategy for both new and existing consumers, marketers first must fully understand the factors leading them to make the purchase. This is where the cognitive dissonance theory takes part.

What causes Cognitive dissonance

- **Forced cognitive behavior**: When you don't want to do something but due to some pressure you are bound to do something against your beliefs. For example - In an organizational buying process the top management decision was generally given preference. The final user of the product is middle-level management or the subordinates in that situation the subordinate may feel cognitive dissonance due to forced cognitive behavior.
- **Decision making (Choice between A & B)**: When we have to make a choice between two alternatives that are equally good then we always face dissonance. For example - While purchasing cosmetic products people usually get puzzles, people are not able to evaluate the alternative, and finally, people may face mental discomfort after buying.
- **Effort:** When we put a lot of effort into something later on we realize it's not worth it.

How can we resolve this Cognitive dissonance?

- We can change one of those thoughts. Ex- Someone may believe that smoking is not bad
- We can change the behavior. Ex- one can stop smoking
- Adding new thoughts. Ex- Smoking is bad but I do regular exercise and do a lot of things that are good for my health.
- Ignore one of that thoughts. Ex- I don't care (live life today who has seen the future!)

Steps to improve the post-purchase behavior

Many companies now focus on the customer even after they have bought the product so that the customer can consider the brand again in the future. The entire customer relationship management is based on this. Below are some of the steps which can be taken to improve the behavior.

1. Proper Customer Service and Support Channels: In case the customer needs to understand or talk to someone about the product after buying, the company should provide clear channels like a contact center, knowledge, service portals, etc. so that customer can contact us in case an issue arises. This way customers would have a clear path to take in case there is some issue with the bought product or service. Sometimes the issues can be minor and easily solvable through support.

2. User Manual and Knowledge Portal: Proper product documentation and manual should be provided with products, especially which require high involvement like vacuum cleaners, cars, and appliances so that customers can refer them to resolve an issue. A help portal can go long way in resolving issues automatically

3. Returns Management: Customers should be assured that in case the product is not working as per their expectations they can always return it. The company should clearly define the processes in case of return so that the experience is good in case the customer chooses to return.

4. Understand customer feedback: It is very important to understand what the customers are saying about the products and services. A company should try to gather feedback from customers and use it to improve the products so that next time, less number of customers are dissatisfied.

Innovation

According to Peter Drucker "This is a new era of opportunity, but only for those who are willing to accept change as an opportunity, not for those who are afraid of it". The business environment is changing day by day due to the advancement of new technology, new ideas, new innovations. In this era, only those organizations can sustain themselves in the market and is ready to accept the change.

Innovation is the search for and discovery, development, improvement, adaptation, and commercialization of new processes, products, and organization structures and procedures. It is an ideal practice or object that is perceived as new by an individual or other unit of adaptation. In business, the new invention must have commercialization to be a successful innovation. Because without commercialization innovation was meaningless. While working on innovation there is an object or problem that is being changed. It can be a product, a process an individual lifestyle, an organization strategy a society culture. Innovation may vary in extent or magnitude i.e. degree to which one derives from the past. It is closely related to problem-solving since the generation and implementation of ideas for change never transpire without difficulties and the final characteristic is the impact of change, the significance or range of its effect.

Goals of Innovations

Following are the few goals of innovations-

1. Improving quality
2. Creation of new markets.
3. Extension of the product range.
4. Improving production process
5. Reducing wastage of materials.
6. Reducing environmental damages.
7. Reducing energy consumption.

Types of Innovations

Innovations can be classified into three types-

- **Continuous innovation:** In this type of innovation continuous modification or improvement of existing products. For example- New or advanced models of cars. i10 ,i20.
- **Dynamically continuous:** This is a type of innovation that involves the creation of new products or the alteration of existing ones, but does not generally alter published patterns of customer buying and product use.
- **Discontinuous innovations:** This is nothing but the production of a completely new product that causes customers to alter their behavioral patterns significantly.

Diffusion of Innovation

One of the earliest social science theories is the Diffusion of Innovation theory, which was created by E.M. Rogers in 1962. It first appeared in communication to describe how an idea or product gathers steam and diffuses (or spreads) within a particular population or social system over time. As a result of this spread, people adopt a new idea, habit, or product as part of a social system. When someone adopts, they do something that is different from what they previously did (i.e., purchase or use a new product, acquire and perform a new behavior, etc.). Adoption depends on a person's ability to see an idea, behavior, or product as novel or inventive. This allows for the possibility of dissemination. In simple words the diffusion of innovation, theory seeks to explain how and why new ideas and practices are adopted with timelines potentially spread out over a long time.

There are five established adopter categories. These are **innovators, early adopters, early majority, late majority, and laggards.** When promoting an invention to a specific demographic, it is critical to identify the features of that population that will enhance or limit the acceptance of the innovation. Although the bulk of the general population tends to fall towards the middle of the five established adopter categories, it is still important to comprehend the traits of the target demographic. Various tactics are employed while advertising innovation to appeal to the various adopter segments.

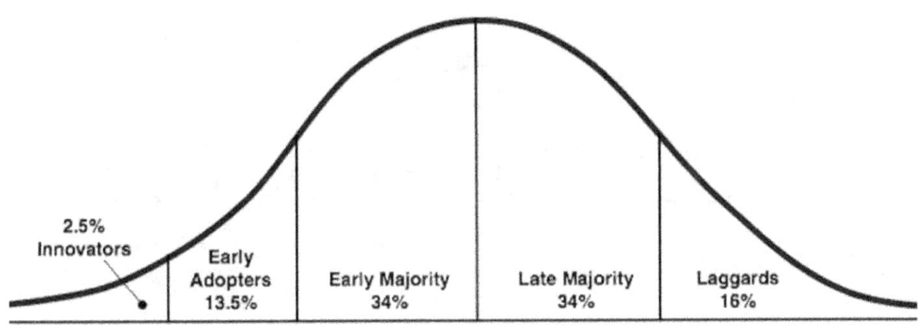

Exhibit 2.3: Diffusion of Innovation

Innovators - These are people who want to be the first to try the innovation. They are venturesome and interested in new ideas. These people are very willing to take risks and are often the first to develop new ideas. Very little, if anything, needs to be done to appeal to this population.

Early Adopters - These are people who represent opinion leaders. They enjoy leadership roles and embrace change opportunities. They are already aware of the need to change and so are very comfortable adopting new ideas. Strategies to appeal to this population include how-to manuals and information sheets on implementation. They do not need the information to convince them to change.

Early Majority - These people are rarely leaders, but they do adopt new ideas before the average person. That said, they typically need to see evidence that the innovation works before they are willing to adopt it. Strategies to appeal to this population include success stories and evidence of the innovation's effectiveness.

Late Majority - These people are skeptical of change, and will only adopt an innovation after it has been tried by the majority. Strategies to appeal to this population include information on how many other people have tried the innovation and have adopted it successfully.

Laggards - These people are bound by tradition and very conservative. They are very skeptical of change and are the hardest group to bring on board. Strategies to appeal to this population include statistics, fear appeals, and pressure from people in the other adopter groups.

CHAPTER THREE

Models of Buying Behavior

**"*Learning Objective*

- *Models of Consumer Behaviour.*
- *Rationality in purchase.*
- *Emotional purchase*

Lorose

Consumer Behavior Model

A model is simply a means of describing a concept, its causes, and its effects. . By using these models, we can map out each cause or antecedent of a particular behavior and each of its results or consequences. As we have seen, there are numerous elements that influence consumer decision-making. In order to understand consumer behavior, there are many consumer models available. Consumer behavior models are instrumental in understanding how, when, and why customers buy.

Consumer behavior models are divided into two types: the traditional model and the Contemporary model. In traditional models, we have Economic Model, Psychoanalytic Model, Learning Model, and Sociological model. Whereas in Contemporary Model we have Howard Sheth Model, Nicosia Model, Stimulus-Response Model, and Engel, Blackwell, and Minard Model. Let's discuss these models one by one-

Economic Model:

The Economic Model is one of the oldest models of Consumer Behaviour and tries to explain what a person is likely to buy and in what quantity. This model takes into consideration the behavior of an economic man, who would give foremost importance to monetary or financial considerations while making a decision. The ultimate objective of an individual, as per this model, is the maximization of satisfaction by investing the minimum money resources for the satisfaction of needs and wants. In short, we can conclude that this model focus on the " Act of Purchase" of an Average Consumer. Explains " What" a consumer would purchase and In what quantity? According to the economic model of consumer behavior, consumers try to maximize the utility of products on the basis of the law of diminishing marginal utility. The desire of consumers to obtain maximum gains by spending a minimum amount acts as the core for the derivation of this model.

Despite having certain limitations, it is one of the widely used models of consumer behavior and is a must-know for all students of marketing and business management.

Learning Model:

This model is based on the idea that consumer behavior is governed by the need to satisfy basic and learned needs. Basic needs include food, clothing, and shelter, and learned needs fear and guilt. Thus, a consumer will have a tendency to buy things that will satisfy their needs and provide satisfaction. For example- A hungry customer may pass up on buying a nice piece of jewellery to buy some food, but will later go back to purchase the jewellery once his hunger is satisfied. This model takes influence from psychologist Abraham Maslow's Hierarchy of Needs (Exhibit 3.1). The bottom level of this hierarchy represents basic needs, and ascending sections describe learned needs, or secondary desires, that allow consumers to feel as though they've reached self-fulfillment.

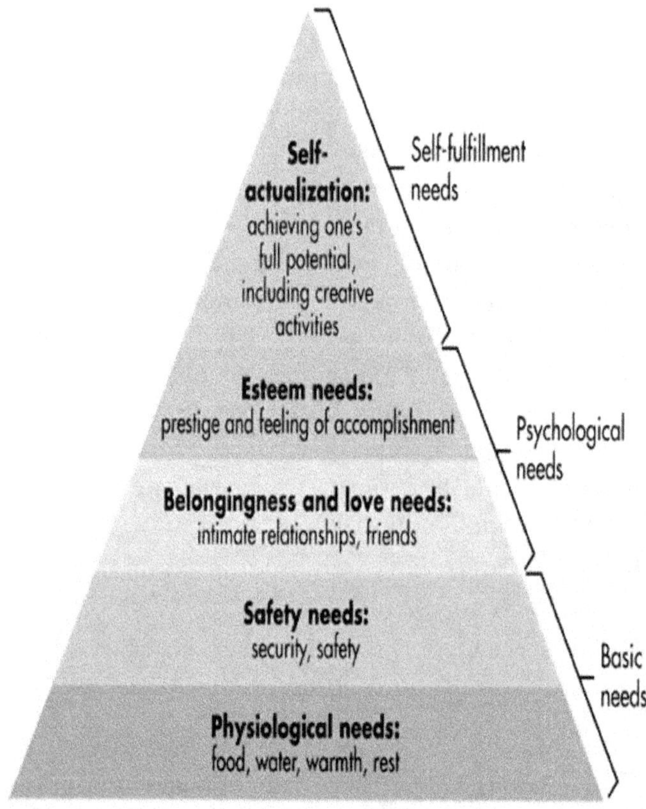

Exhibit 3.1: Mashlows Need Hierarchy Theory

Psychoanalytical Model:

This model takes into consideration the fact that consumer behavior is influenced by both the conscious and the subconscious mind. The three levels of consciousness discussed by Sigmund Freud (id, ego, superego) all work to influence one's buying decisions and behavior. Here id is the all characteristics that an individual is born with. Superego is formed out of values and the ego acts as a balance between the id and the superego.

This model is concerned with personality and says that human behavior to a great extent is directed by a complex set of deep-seated motives that helps the marketer to know how buyers are influenced by symbolic factors in buying a product. A hidden symbol in a company's name or logo may have an effect on a person's subconscious mind and may influence him to buy that product instead of a similar product from another company. For example - In today's market there are a number of fake products which are true copies of original products. These brands is having almost everything same packaging, product features, quantity, etc. only a little change in the logo or brand name is visible but the customer's subconscious mind believes that even if the product is fake they believe the product is the real one. Because maybe the customer is not aware of that or they are not having sufficient time for the examination of the product.

Sociological Model:

As per this model, an individual buyer is a part of the institution called society, gets influenced by it, and in the turn, also influences it in its path of development. The interactions with all the sets of society leave some impression on him and may play a role in influencing his buying behavior. Marketers, through a process of market segmentation, can work out the common behavior patterns of a specific class and group of buyers and try to influence their buying patterns. Family, friends, and close associates exert the maximum influence. Opinion leader influences the lifestyle and buying behavior of an individual. For example -Medical representatives are expected to be professional and formal. People who hold these jobs will make purchases that speak to and uphold this group's rules, like formal business wear. This model can apply to most businesses, especially those that create products and services relevant to specific groups.

Howard Sheth Model:

This is one of the models that represent consumer behavior in the market. It attempts to explain the rationality of choice of the products by the consumer under conditions of incomplete information and reduced processing capacity. This model is slightly complicated and shows that consumer behavior is a complex process and concepts of learning, perception, and attitudes influence consumer behavior. This model of decision-making is applicable to individuals. It has four sets of variables which are:

- Input variables
- Output Variables
- Hypothetical constructs - Perceptual constructs, and learning constructs
- Exogenous variables.

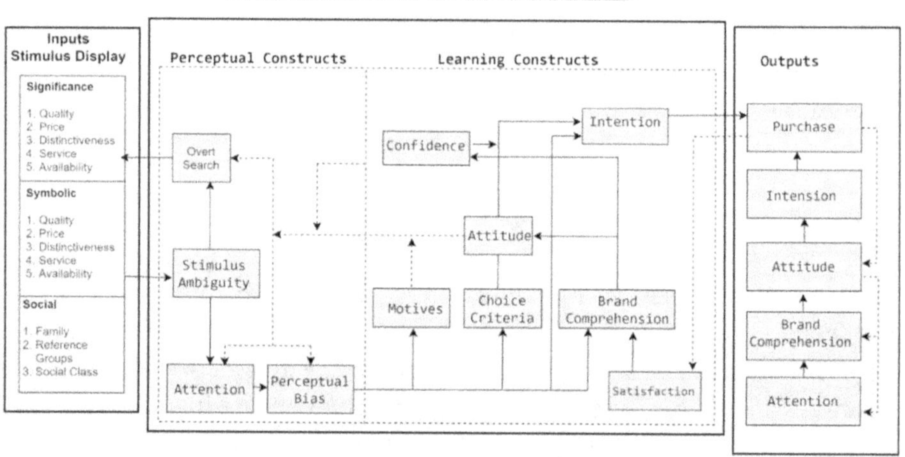

Exhibit 3.2: Howard Sheth Model

Inputs: Some inputs are necessary for the customer for making decisions. These inputs are provided by three types of stimuli as shown in Exhibit 3.2.

(a) Significative stimuli: These are physical tangible characteristics of the product. These are price, quality, distinctiveness, services rendered, and availability of the product. These are essential for making decisions.

(b) Symbolic stimuli: These are the same as significative characteristics, but they include the perception of the individual, i.e., price is high or low. Quality is up to the mark or below average. How is it different from the other products, what services can the product render and, what is the position of after-sales service and how quickly or easily is the product available and, from where.

(c) Social stimuli: This is the stimulus provided by family, friends, social groups, and social class. This is important, as one lives in society and for the approval and appreciation of society, buying habits have to be governed.

Hypothetical constructs - Perceptual constructs, and learning constructs: These constructs are psychological variables, e.g., motives, attitudes, and perception which influence the consumer decision process. The consumer receives the stimuli and interprets them. Two factors that influence his interpretation are stimulus ambiguity and perpetual bias. Stimulus ambiguity occurs when the consumer cannot interpret or fully understand the meaning of the stimuli he has received and does not know how to respond. Perceptual bias occurs when an individual distorts the information according to his needs and experiences. These two factors influence the individual for the comprehension and rating of the brand. If the brand is rated high, he develops confidence in it and finally purchases it.

Output: By output, we mean the purchase decision. After purchase, there is satisfaction or dissatisfaction.
Satisfaction leads to a positive attitude and increases brand comprehension. With dissatisfaction, a negative attitude is developed. The feedback shown by the dotted line and the solid lines shows the flow of information.

Exogenous or External variables: These are not shown in the model, and do not directly influence the decision process. They influence the consumer indirectly and vary from one consumer to another. These are the individual's own personality traits, social class, the importance of the purchase, and financial status. All four factors discussed above are dependent on each other and influence the decision-making process. The model though complicated deals with the purchase behavior in an exhaustive manner.

Nicosia Model:

This model shows the interactive relationship between the company and the customer. They arise between them for mutual communication – the company communicates with consumers through promotional activities, while consumers by making purchases. This model explains consumer behavior on the basis of four fields shown in the diagram. The output of field one becomes the input of field two, and so on. This model explains consumer behavior on the basis of four fields shown in the diagram. The output of field one becomes the input of field two, and so on.

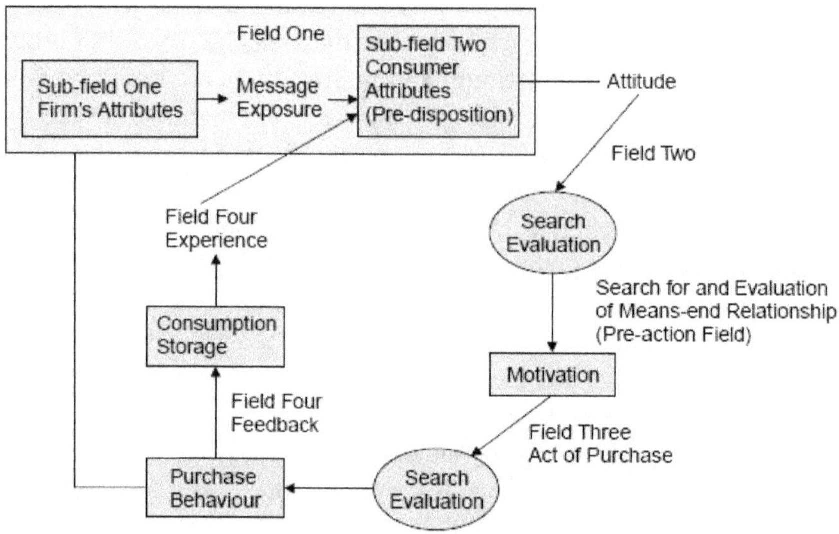

Exhibit 3.3: Nicosia Model of Consumer Behavior

Field one consists of subfields one and two. Subfield one is the firm's attributes and the attributes of the product. Subfield two is the predisposition of the consumer and his own characteristics and attributes, which are affected by his exposure to various information and message, and is responsible for the building of the attitude of the consumer.

Field two is the preaction field, where the consumer goes on for research and evaluation and gets motivated to buy the product. It highlights the means and end relationship. Field three is the act of purchase or the decision-making to buy the product. The customer buys the product and uses it. Field four highlights the post-purchase behavior and the use of the product, its storage, and consumption. The feedback from field four is fed into the firm's attributes or field one, and the feedback from the experience is responsible for changing the pre-disposition of the consumer and later his attitude towards the product. Nicosia Model is a comprehensive model dealing with all aspects of building attitudes, purchase, and use of products including the post-purchase behavior of the consumer.

Engel-Blackwell-Kollat Model:

It consists of four components:
(i) Information processing
(ii) Central control unit
(iii) Decision process
(iv) Environmental influences.

Information processing: As shown in the diagram information processing consists of exposure, attention, comprehension, and retention of the marketing and non-marketing stimuli. For successful sales, the consumer must be properly and repeatedly exposed to the message. His attention should be
drawn, such that he understands what is to be conveyed and retains it in his mind.

Central control unit: The stimuli process and interprets the information received by an individual. This is done with the help of four psychological factors.
(a) Stores information and past experience about the product, which serves as a standard for comparing other products and brands.
(b) Evaluative criteria which could be different for different individuals.
(c) Attitudes or the state of mind which changes from time to time, and helps in choosing
the product.
(d) The personality of the consumer which guides him to make a choice suiting his personality.

Decision process: In this model of consumer they view consumer behavior as a decision-making process and identify five activities occurring in this decision process over a period of time. The decision outcome or the satisfaction and dissatisfaction is also an important factor that influences further decisions. The decision process may involve extensive problem-solving, limited problem-solving, or routinized response behavior. This depends on the type and value of the product to be purchased.

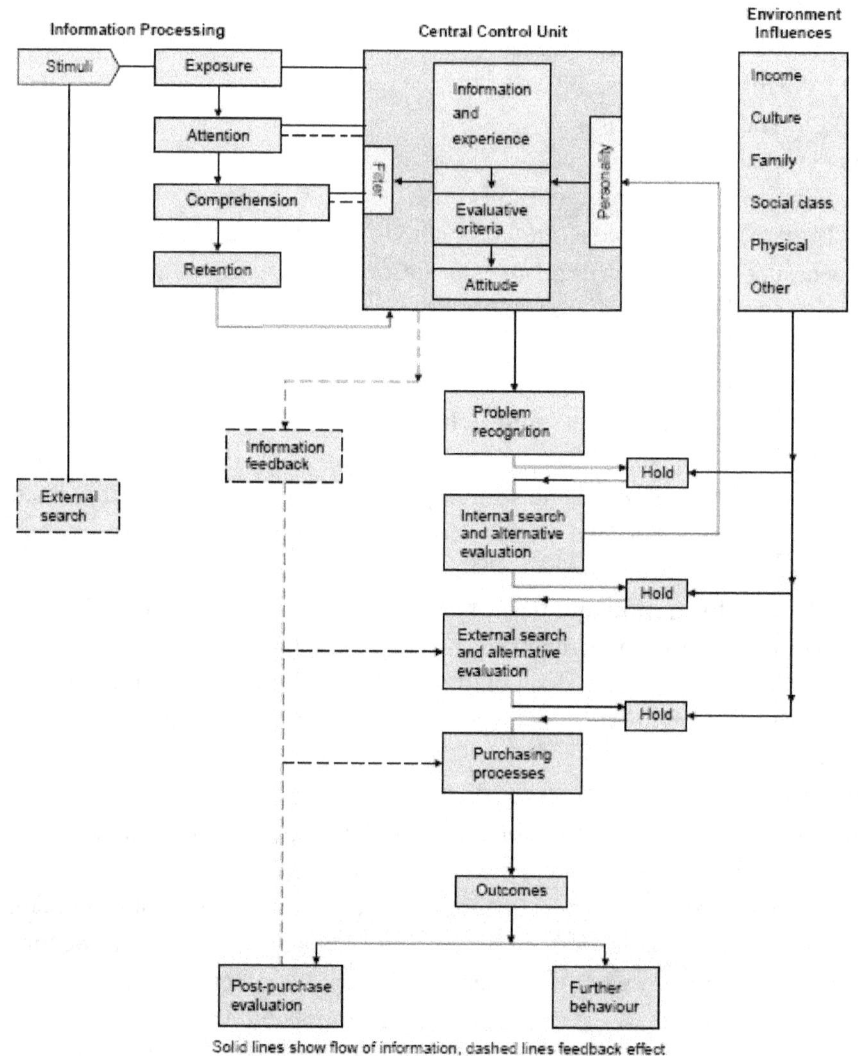

Exhibit 3.4: Engel-Blackwell-Kollat Model

Environmental influences: The environmental influences are also shown in a separate box and consist of income, social class, family influences, social class, physical influences, and other considerations. All these factors may favor or disfavor the purchase decisions.

<u>RATIONALITY IN PURCHASE</u>

Rational Purchase: Rational purchases are those purchases that are mainly based on objective criteria:

- Profit
- Security
- Utility
- Caution
- Health

For these, rational factors outweigh emotional ones. For example-We buy health insurance because we want to ensure getting the best possible treatment in the first place. Our emotional mindset towards the provider is secondary.

These purchases follow the five stages of consumer behavior mentioned before very strictly:

1. An urgent need is recognized ("My car is broken, I need a new one.")
2. Extensive research ("Which companies/ brands offer the desired product?")
3. Evaluation of alternatives ("Which brand offers the most value? Which model fits my needs? Which company has the lowest prices?")
4. Purchase decision ("I will buy a Mercedes-Benz C-Class")
5. Post-purchase evaluation (Dissonance: "This car does not fit my needs."/ Delight: "This car offers the best value for money.")
6. Rational purchases are accompanied by extensive research and comparisons of different products and offers. Pages like Amazon or price-comparison portals specialize in offering both an extensive range of products and detailed information on the products.
7. In general, rational purchases are made for products that require in-depth research, information, and more extensive knowledge. Oftentimes, the products require higher expenses and a deeper level of dedication.
8. A car, for example, is not purchased without comparing different models beforehand, and running shoes have to fit the need of the consumer

(beginner or advanced level?), as these are products that are used over a longer period of time, require spending a higher amount of money and need to perform well to satisfy the consumer's needs. Therefore, these purchases are not at all based on impulses and cannot be triggered as easily as emotional purchases can be.

Emotional Purchase: Neuroscientists emphasize that emotions play a central role in our decision-making progress: Neuroscientist Antonio Damasio conducted a study that found that people who were unable to generate emotions due to medical conditions had trouble making decisions.

Criteria which impact emotional purchase decisions are highly personal like- Love/sentiment, Envy, Pride, Entertainment, Vanity

For emotional purchase decisions, it can be argued that the need does not necessarily have to be present in the first place. It is rather created by external sources, like influencers. Thus, these purchase decisions are strongly based on impulses as well as recommendations. There is not a long-term need or an urgent circumstance that leads to purchasing a product. The customer does not look for information prior to the purchase and does not evaluate alternatives. The decision is purely based on emotional input.

Consumer Involvement and Satisfaction

- *Consumer Involvement*
- *Consumer Satisfaction*
- *Brand equity and brand loyalty.*

Lorose

Consumer Involvement:

Consumer involvement refers to the degree of information processing or extent of importance that a consumer attaches to a product. The degree of involvement has a very significant effect on consumer behavior. When more expensive products are to be purchased, the consumer gets more involved in the purchase process but he may not be equally involved in a product that is just a rupee or two priced. For example, if a consumer wants to buy a packet of tea or food or bread or butter he does not feel very much involved. It is because the life of these products is very short and once consumed they exhaust. If the experience with the product is not good, another brand can be purchased next time. However, this is not true in the case of consumer durables and certain services. If one buys an automobile, refrigerator, air conditioner, furniture, or a house, he is forced to use it for a long period and cannot change early and if he decides to dispose of it, there is a big loss. Hence in these products, there is a high degree of involvement, therefore, the consumer takes a decision after a lot of deliberations. In the case of insurance policy ones taken, one has to live with it. Thus there are three sets of factors that decided the factor of involvement. These are -Personal Factors, and Object Factors, Situational Factors.

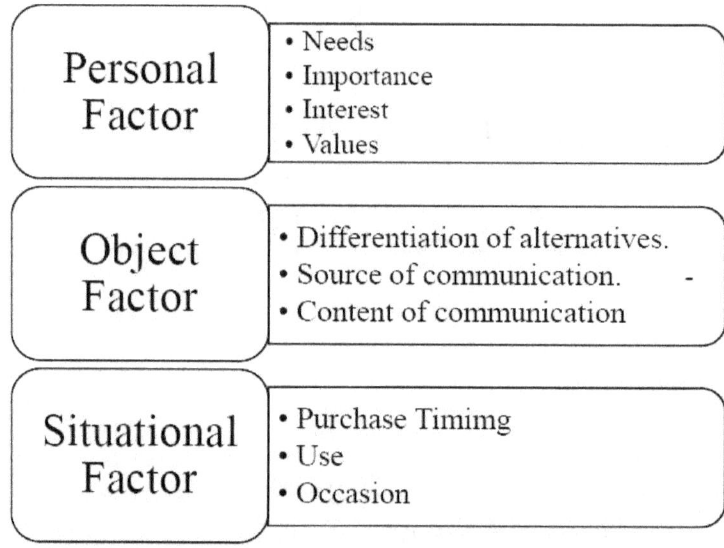

Exhibit 4.1: Factors affecting consumer involvement.

Personal Factors: A person's perceptions, beliefs, attitudes, and values can substantially influence his or her experience and involvement with products. For example, certain cultures highly discourage women from exposing some of their body parts as part of their religious beliefs, which inevitably affects their clothing consumption. Other examples of cultural influences include language, myths, customs, rituals, and laws. Consumers tend to be more involved with products that they believe can fill their own needs, which in turn are regarded as holding importance and relevance in their lives. Personal or individual factors can also strongly influence gender, age, income level or social class, ethnicity, and sexual orientation.

Object Factors: The degree of information that consumers have about a product, including how well they can distinguish its characteristics, can also affect their experience, involvement, and satisfaction. Typically, the higher a consumer's product knowledge, the more involved with it he or she will be. Deeper knowledge about a product also translates into higher involvement because the consumer perceives it as more important, especially if some of that knowledge pertains to characteristics that hold personal meaning.

Situational Factors: Products that can easily conform to and enrich a consumer's lifestyle tend to be consumed with more frequency and involvement. For example, a busy working mother might rely heavily on her smartphone to keep her organized and effective in an effortless manner.

Consumer involvement in the marketing and consumer behavior literature grew out of the realization that much of consumer behavior does not involve an extensive search for information or a comprehensive evaluation of choice alternatives. The consumer makes dozens of mundane decisions and choices each day and it is inappropriate to assume consumers actively process and think about each decision. In this domain, many studies looked at the act of purchase, in addition to the product category itself, and determined the situations of the purchase were highly influential in determining the level of consumer decision-making activity. The degree of involvement depends upon past history of the buyer i.e. his level of knowledge, information, psychology, culture, lifestyle, and social system. Depending upon the circumstance of an individual his involvement differs even for the same service or product. There is no universal and clear-cut acceptable methodology to identify consumer involvement.

Types of Consumer Involvement:

The level of consumer participation in purchasing decisions is influenced by a number of factors. Their level of education, information, psychology, culture, way of life, social structure, etc. are a few examples. Depending on the situation, an individual's level of involvement can change even for the same good or service. Five different kinds of involvement exist. They are - ego involvement, commitment, communication in involvement, Purchase importance, and Extent of information.

1. **Ego Involvement:** Ego involvement is done to satisfy one's ego. For example, the entire family may participate in the purchase of a particular item for a single family member. Both the woman and the husband participate in the shopping process: the wife buys clothes for her husband, and the husband buys his wife cosmetics. The family's sons and daughters have a big influence in what the family buys, like a laptop, TV, automobile, or furniture for the house. Each family member's ego is stroked by having input prior to the purchase.

2. **Commitment:** Another significant type of involvement is commitment. The other family members are committed to making arrangements for

medical care for the ailing members of the family when they get ill. Similarly, family commitment is required for events like marriages.

3. **Communication Involvement:** Communication engagement is the act of informing people within the family or organization of the information that is already available. If one member has some information on the subject matter of the decision, he should communicate it with the other members before arriving at a decision.

4. **Purchase Importance:** The involvement of individuals depends upon the degree of importance of the purchase. Suppose e flat costing lakhs of rupees is purchased, then the purchase decision assumes a great deal of importance in respect of the location and area of the flat. The title deeds should be free from encumbrance.

5. **The extent of information:** Once the consumer recognizes the need, he then engages in a search process. Search means the acquisition of information from the environment. The extent of the information search is part of purchase importance. When the purchase is important, information is sought from all possible sources. But in the case of routine purchases of products and services, information search will be rather minimal.

Level of Involvement

Involvement levels are divided into three types **Low involvement, High involvement**, and **Some involvement**. Some low-involvement products are habitual items and low-price products. but there all low-price items do not come with low involvement levels like medicine when a medicine is being purchased, which may not be very expensive, yet the customer may be highly involved in checking that it shouldn't react him. Books also came in this category. The book purchased by a student for preparing competitive exam may not be as expensive as a car, yet the customer gets highly involved because it is an important product.

Ways to Increase Involvement Levels: The degree of involvement, whether it be low, high, or limited, differs by the consumer but less so by product. The degree to which a consumer engages with a given product will depend on their background, level of product expertise, and method of information gathering in general. But in a competitive market, brands are constantly striving for the preference, allegiance, and approval of consumers. To improve exposure, attention, and relevance, many firms will employ marketing methods; in other words, brands are continuously looking for ways to inspire consumers with the goal of boosting consumer involvement with their goods and services. Some of the different ways marketers increase consumer involvement are: customization; engagement; incentives etc.

- Customization: Customization allows users to make choices and define preferences in a system, giving them more control over their user experience. Users can choose the content, layout, functionality, or design that they like due to customization. However, because customization tools demand effort and input from users, they must be created in a way that encourages use and offers a sufficient return on the user's investment.
- Engagement: The technique and content needed to generate meaningful customer interactions and promote brand loyalty is engagement marketing. It uses an inbound marketing strategy that is cross-channel and consists of various marketing campaigns like email marketing, content marketing, social media marketing, marketing automation, etc.
- Incentives: Customer loyalty and reward programs effectively influence consumer decisions and establish purchase patterns. An incentive is a specific strategy to persuade people by giving them something to achieve an objective. Incentive marketing is also used to dispose of inventory or to push slow-moving products. Nonetheless, incentive marketing is an effective tool to increase sales and consumer involvement.

Strategic implication of low involvement decision making: In case of low involvement decision making, it is more likely that the consumer changes the brand in the market or there is a bargain sale or discount sale. In low-involvement products, consumers usually don't have any brand loyalty and may be easily shifted to other competitive brands whose price is lower.

Types of Involvement media: Like the level of involvement. Involvement media also can be divided into two types. i.e. High involvement media, Low involvement media.

- High-involvement media: Print media such as newspapers & magazines are high-involvement media because the information is processed clearly leading to attitude formation and finally behavior.
- Low involvement media: TV is a low involvement media because it is primarily pictorial, allowing viewers passive and holistic processing of

information.

Major dimensions of Involvement:

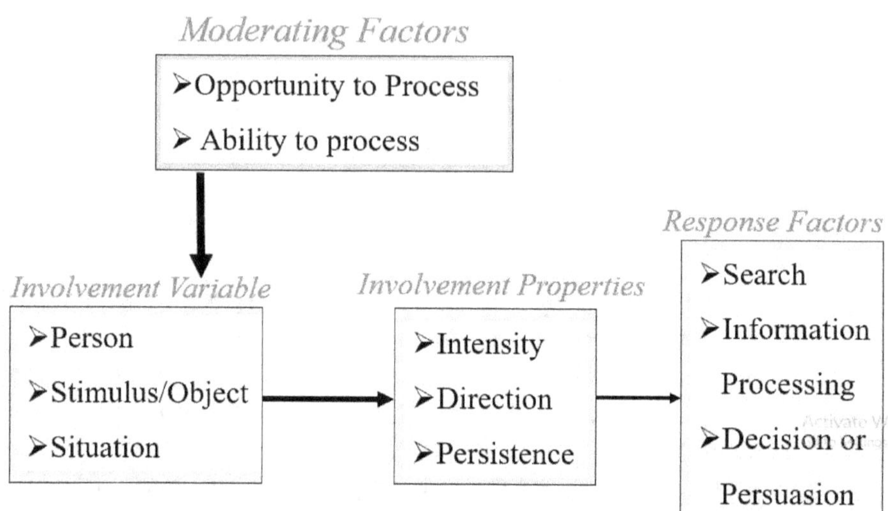

Exhibit 4.1: Major dimension of Involvement

1. **Moderating Factors:** Moderating factors are those which may limit the opportunity & the ability to process the information and influence the level of involvement. For example, a consumer is planning to purchase a mobile phone & the commercial he is watching would be quite interesting to him. Suddenly somebody knocks on the door & which distracts his attention from the ad and the consumer may not possess much knowledge about a particular product and fails to understand some of the information contained in the ad. So this would limit the evaluation of alternative brands in a satisfactory manner. From this example, we understand that opportunity to process the information and the ability to process the information plays a crucial role in the consumer involvement process.

2. **Involvement Variables:** Involvement variables are like persons or objects that may also affect the consumer involvement process.

   Person- The variable related to person refers to personal needs, values, interests & experiences, etc. For example, a person interested in computers is very likely to have a personal interest in computer-related magazines to learn about new development. **Stimulus or object** refers to a product or stimuli that the consumer perceives to be closely related to his/her values, experience, and interest. For example in the case of computers, one should not expect the same level of involvement for all consumers.

3. **Involvement Properties:** Intensity, Direction, and Persistence also affect consumer involvement. Involvement intensity refers to the severity of involvement as experienced by the consumer and is generally categorized as high or low. Direction refers to the focus of involvement and involvement variables will strongly affect this focus. The focus could be a product, service, and or purchase decision. Persistence describes the length of time the consumer remains involved with the purchase decision.

4. **Response Factor:** Response factors concern how a consumer behaves under involvement conditions of different intensity. These factors include different patterns of information search, information processing, evaluation of alternatives, and post-decision actions. One may expect that consumer who is high in enduring involvement for a product will undertake regular, ongoing search for information & low involvement will result in little search for information.

Role of Consumer Involvement in Consumer decision making

Some consumers are characterized as being more involved in products and shopping than others. A consumer who is highly involved with a product would be interested in knowing a lot about it before purchasing. Hence he reads brochures thoroughly, compares brands and models available at different outlets, asks questions, and looks for recommendations. Thus consumer involvement is an inner urge that creates within an individual an interest to hold certain products/services offering in greater importance.

Involvement possesses certain properties-

- The degree of involvement may vary from high and low. A highly involved consumer would actively search for information and collect facts, comparing the various brands. On the other hand low involvement customers.

- The length of time that the consumer remains in this heightened state determines the level of persistence. It could be short-term and situational interest in the product or it could be long-term and enduring.
- It is directed towards any or all of the elements of the marketing mix. A person may show involvement towards the products(their feature, attribute) the price, the store, or promotional efforts.

A mechanism underlines the very process of involvement. As a process, involvement is impacted by certain "antecedents" that get restrained by "moderating factors" and finally affect its degree of intensity and level of persistence. The level of involvement reflects how personally important the consumer purchase the product or service, how interested the customer is in consuming a product, and how much information he wants before making a purchase decision. As high-involvement products have characteristics like the emotional risk of the customer, and projection of self -----So, A sales presentation must be good enough to offer highly involved products by understanding the emotional needs of the customer.

Consumer Satisfaction

Customer satisfaction is a measure of how well a company's products and services meet customers' expectations. It reflects your business' health by showing how well your products are resonating with buyers. Consumer satisfaction may be defined as the products and service performance according to the buyer's expectations. Customer expectation depends on the product's actual performance relative to buyer expectation but buyer expectations rely on the customer's past buying experience. So marketers must be careful to set the right level of expectation. Levels of customer satisfaction are (in respect of service) ideal level of service, normal level of service, experience-based expectation, acceptable level of expectation, adequate level of expectation, and tolerable level of expectation.

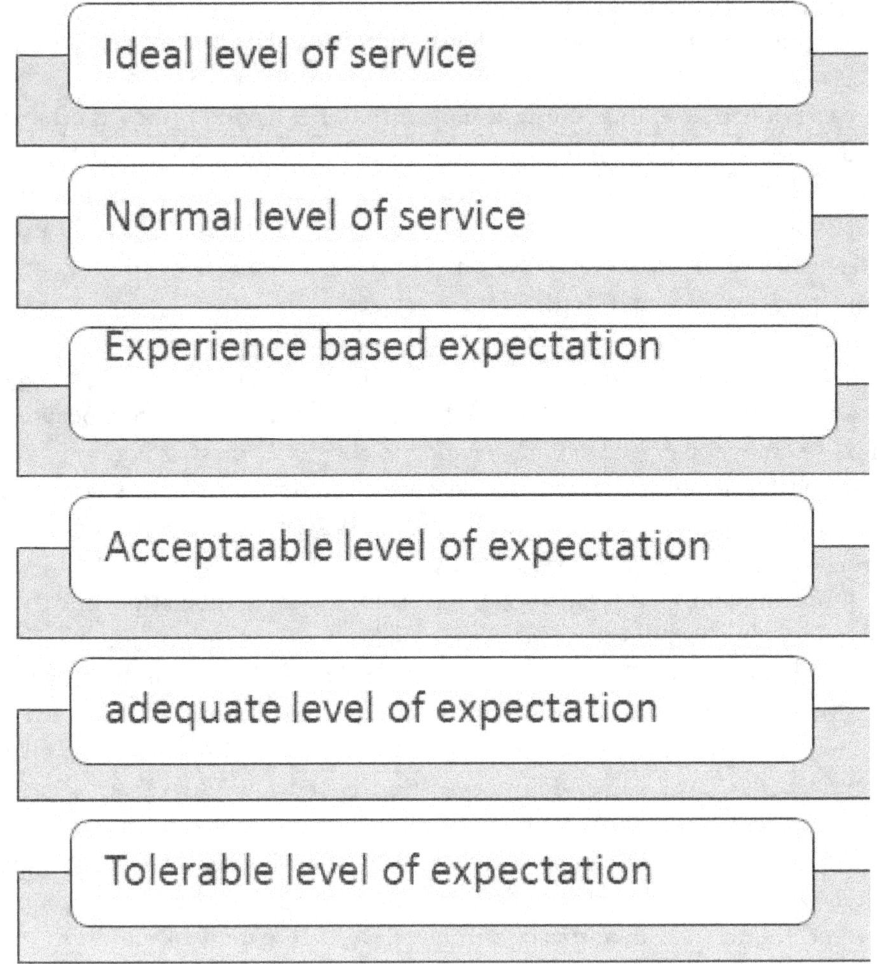

Exhibit 4.2: Level of consumer expectations

The ideal level of service: This is the highest level of service expectation. But customers usually don't expect this level of service because it rarely takes place. Ideal expectations refer to the performance wished for in perfect service. Desired expectations are the performance levels that customers want the service to meet in practice. If the service provider cannot deliver service at the desired level, customers may be willing to tolerate deviations in performance up to their acceptable expectations with a relatively small degradation in satisfaction. Dissatisfaction results if the performance falls below this level.

The normal level of service: This is the normal level of service that everyone received. This level of service is fair treatment.

Experience level expectation: If a consumer is having prior experience enjoying a particular service he may expect the same level of satisfaction the next time. So this level of expectation is totally dependent upon the past experience of the consumer. Past experience includes experience with a particular service vendor, experience with other vendors within the same industry, and experience with related services.

Acceptable level of expectation: This is the OK level of service.

The adequate level of expectation: This is the minimum level of service that a consumer may accept. Service below this level may lead to a negative impression in consumers' minds, leading to consumer dissatisfaction.

Tolerable level of service: This is the minimum level of service that a consumer may accept for the first time. But consumer retention is not at all possible with this level of consumer expectation.

From the above, we can broadly classify service expectation into two categories **Desired level of service expectation** and **Adequate level of service expectation. The desired** level of service expectation is nothing but it is the level of service that a customer expected to receive. Basically, it is a mental expectation of customers that he hopes and wishes to receive. The adequate level of service expectation is the level of service that a customer will accept, this is the minimum tolerable level that a customer can accept. If the consumer received service above the desired level then he felt delighted and if the consumer received service below the adequate level of expectation then dissatisfaction may arise. The extent of variation the customer recognized and are willing to accept is called **Zone of tolerance.** For higher customer satisfaction every marketer must understand the desired level of customer expectations so that they can narrow down the zone of tolerance.

<table>
<tr><td>

ADEQUATE SERVICE

ZONE OF TOLERANCE

ADEQUATE SERVICE

</td></tr>
</table>

Exhibit 4.2: Zone of Tolerance

Levels of customer satisfaction:

Customers are the backbone of business; as a result, they should be considered the market's king. Customers are essential to the organization's growth, profitability, status, and other aspects of the business. Therefore, it is crucial for all businesses to satisfy all of their clients and prove that they are happy consumers. The levels of customer satisfaction are-

- Level One: Meeting Customer Expectations
- Level Two: Surpassing Customer Expectations
- Level Three: Delighting your Customers
- Level Four: Amazing your Customers

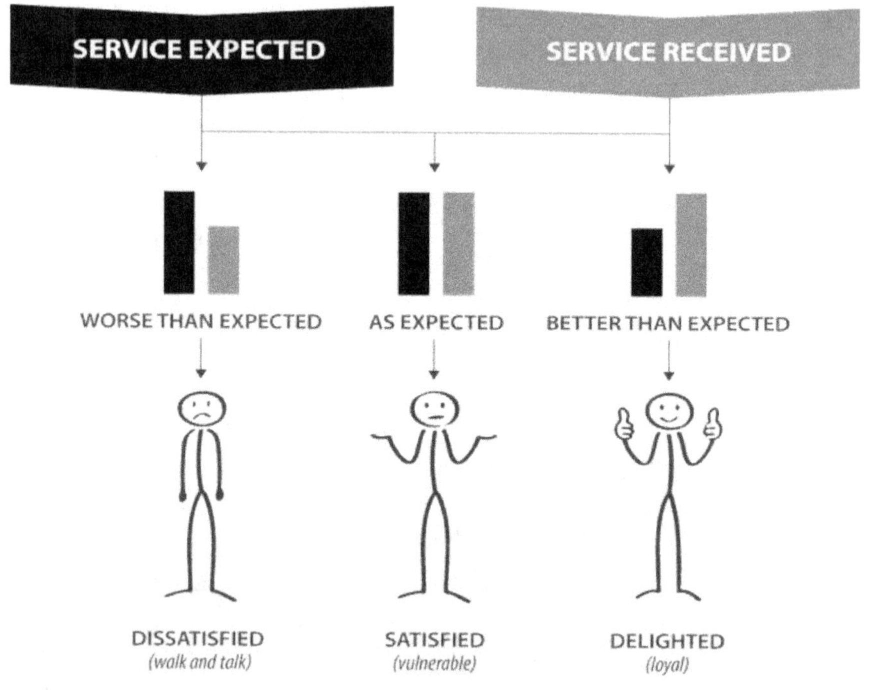

Exhibit 4.3: Customer satisfaction

Determinants of Customer Satisfaction: There are three determinants of customer satisfaction. They are Basic needs, Performance needs, and Excitement needs.

- Basic needs: These are the basic features of a particular product or service. The presence of these features does not lead to customer satisfaction. But the absence of these basic features may cause severe customer dissatisfaction. For example -In a car, the door lock facility is the basic feature of any car. The presence of a door lock facility does not contribute to customer satisfaction but the absence of this door lock facility may cause huge customer dissatisfaction. These basic needs are also called dissatisfiers.

- Performance needs: It is the need or wants of a customer which he especially asks for. Better the performance more will be customer satisfaction. This factor becomes the benchmark in a competitive market. Performance needs are just working as a satisfier of any product or service. A consumer is usually attracted to a particular product or service only for this special characteristic of the product.

- Excitement needs: A delighter is a consumer's unspoken or unexpected requirement. It leads to a very high level of satisfaction or customer delight. The absence of a delighter doesn't result in customer dissatisfaction while its presence will enhance customer satisfaction.

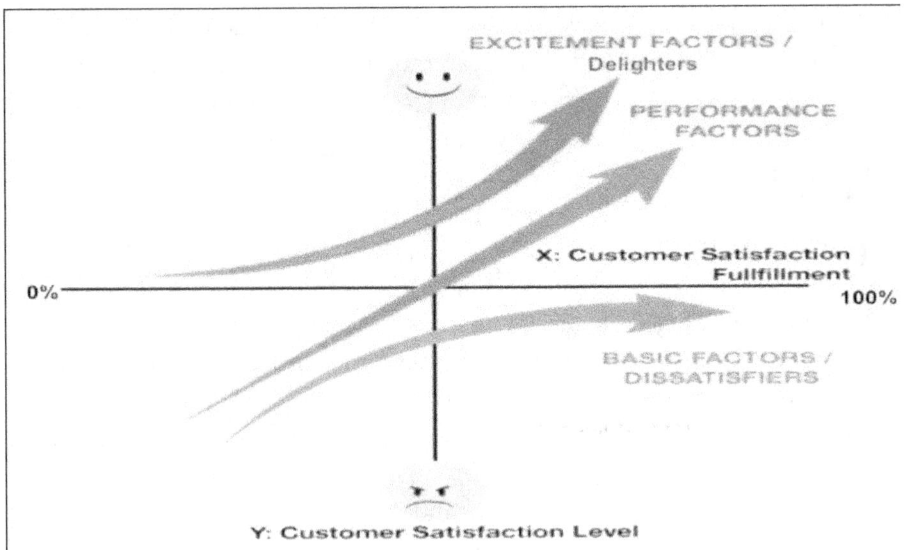

Exhibit 4.3: Graphical representation of determinants of customer satisfaction

Way to measure customer satisfaction: There are various ways to measure customer satisfaction. Following are some of the ways -

1. Survey customers: We can calculate the level of customer satisfaction by undertaking a customer survey at the point of sale.

2. Understanding expectations: Understanding customer expectation is a very crucial part for marketers. As the customer is the king of business it is very much necessary to understand what adjectly customers want from a particular business organization. By calculating customer expectations and what actually a business firm delivers we can also calculate the level of customer satisfaction.

3. Pinpoint specifies: Marketers also collect information on what customer purchase, what they like or they did not like their actual performance expectations, and suggestions for improvement.

4. Loyalty measurement: If a customer recommends a particular product and service to someone that means the customer is satisfied with the particular product or service. A marker can also determine the level of customer satisfaction by determining customers' overall satisfaction, repurchasing, and the likelihood of the products.

5. Intension to repurchase: If a customer is very much happy with any particular brand or product, it is very much likely that the customer may again buy the product. Marketers can track consumer behavior and determine the repurchasing rate and accordingly calculate customer satisfaction.

Brand Equity

American Marketing Association defines **brands** as " A brand is a name, team, sign, symbol, or design or a combination of them intended to identify the goods and services of one seller or group of sellers and to differentiate them from those of competition". A product is something that is made in a factory or any manufacturing premises it is very much easy to copy by any other business firm but a brand is something that is brought by customers which is very much difficult to copy. A brand is unique. A product can be quickly outdated but a successful brand is timeless. In other words, we can say that a brand resides in the minds of customers. A brand can convey up to six levels of meaning. They are Attributes, benefits, values, culture, personality, and user. Brand attributes are what characterize your brand, without looking at what you do or sell. It's the core values and characteristics — your brand's personality traits so to speak. It's what consumers see when looking at your brand as a whole. The main assets of a brand are brand name awareness, brand loyalty, perceived quality, and brand associations. These assets create value in different ways.

Why does brand matter?

For more than a century, branding has been at the heart of marketing. The capacity to establish, maintain, develop, and defend the company's brands is one of the key competencies a marketing professional should have.

- A brand is a promise that the product will perform as per consumer expectations.
- A brand helps make a mark and differentiate products and services from others in the marketplace.
- A brand helps customers to connect with the product and services on an emotional level.
- A brand represents immaterial assets that often have greater financial value than material assets.
- A strong brand can escape price competition since it can command.
- Strong brands attract loyal customers who tend to repetitively purchase from the same brand.
- Normally people believe that a band means lower purchase risk for consumers as they are dealing with a product or service that they are very much known.

Brand equity is the added value that is endowed to products and services. This value may be reflected in how consumers think, feel, and act with respect to the brand, as well as the prices, market share, and profitability that the brands command for the firm. Brand equity is an important intangible asset that has phycological and financial value to the firm. In simple words, brand equity can be defined as a name or symbol used to identify the source of a product. The brand can add significant value when it is well-organized and has a positive association in the mind of customers. This concept is known as brand equity.

CHAPTER FIVE

Trends in Consumer Behavior

"*Learning Objective*

- *Consumer Behaviour in the Indian context.*
- *Data-driven business decisions based on consumer behavior.*

Consumer Behaviour in the Indian context:

Indian consumers' spending habits had evolved during the past few years. Modern customers' purchasing habits are changing due to a number of variables, including urbanization, changing lifestyles, improved consumer knowledge, rising disposable income, shifting demographics, penetration of social media and the internet, and more. This shift in customer purchasing habits has made it extremely difficult for companies that manufacture consumer items to survive and expand. India is a huge country with 120 billion people and more than 120 dialects and different languages and cultures. A major three fourth of the country's population lives in rural areas which contribute one-third of the national income. Usually, the following characteristics are visible in their behavior when purchasing any product or service-

1. Indian consumers are noted for their high degree of value orientation, due to this Indians are labeled as one of the most discerning consumers across the globe. Even luxury brands need to develop a distinctive price strategy to compete in the Indian market. Indian consumers are also believed to have loving, caring, and affectionate values. Products that express feelings and emotions are popular among Indian shoppers.

When consumers deeply invest in purchases and recognize significant differences across brands, they engage in complicated purchasing behavior. Consumers become very involved when a product is expensive, hazardous, rarely bought, and extremely self-expressive. As a result, the customer will go through a learning process where they first draw conclusions about the product, then build attitudes, and finally, make a purchase decision.

2. Indian consumers have a very high family orientation. Normally brands that give much emphasis on family value wine heart of Indian people. In India still, people are having big joints family in village areas. So people use to buy large size items of groceries, packet food like tea, milk, butter, etc. However, Indian urban society is now moving toward the nuclear family still.

3. Indian consumers are also associated with values of nitrating care and affection. But after the new Industrial Policy, 1991 Indian market has undergone many dramatic changes. The economic reformation of India was initiated by Govt. of India in the year 1991 as a result of which many private firms also came into the market and increased their production level.

4. By the end of 2025, most of the Indian population will be below 30 years old. So the choice and product selection trends will be very much dependent upon the product selection trends will be very much depended upon demographics.

5. Earlier India is known for its huge joint families. Due to the huge family size earlier majority of the Indian customer usually buy oversized packages of gross items. But now the majority of Indians have adopted the nuclear family so they buy their groceries or necessary items as per requirement.

6. In earlier days Indian consumers were very much sticking to high-involvement products like cars, bikes, Tv, AC, etc. that they usually don't change these products unless they became damaged but due to the advancement of high living standards and technological adaptation now Indian consumers also buy these high involvement products very frequently with the advancement of technology.

7. Indian consumers when it comes to leisure and entertainment more than half of the Indian consumers prefer watching TV, especially in rural areas.

8. Nowadays, due to their busy schedule, Indians are also becoming very time conservative. They have significantly less time for their family and daily stuff. Due to this reason, the adaptation of fast foods, home delivery of foods, and glossaries also increases.

9. Westernization of Indian culture also adopts many western cultures. But India still doesn't forget its origin culture, values, and ethics. So we can observe that the sale of Indian traditional items is usually very high during the festival season.

10. The internet, apart from being an effective medium of advertisement, is now becoming a place to shop for new young consumers. Selling through the internet which is very popular in the Western world now catching up in India as well. With the increasing work pressure and scarcity of time, Internet shopping offers a convenient and easy option for purchase.

11. Today India is witnessing a dramatic raise in the incidence of lifestyle-related health diseases. Modern lifestyles and a raise in income levels are pushing for better healthcare facilities in the country. The medical equipment industry is growing with Indian hospitals adopting more sophisticated western technology. With the increasing awareness about health and hygiene in India, the market for personal healthcare products is also growing.

Data-driven business decisions based on consumer behavior

Businesses today are becoming more data-driven as technologies advance and data is widely available. Plus, being data-driven can transform an organization in an extremely positive way if done right. Data analytics can help companies understand their customers, analyze ad campaigns, personalize, develop products, and create content strategies. With that in mind, being a data-driven business has many benefits, mostly creating powerful strategies that boost bottom lines. Data-driven decision-making (DDDM) is the process of using data to make informed and verified decisions to drive business growth. By using the right KPIs and tools, companies can overcome biases and make the best managerial rulings that are aligned with their strategies.

Data collection can come from something as simple as a survey sent out to your customer database. Many businesses use data from historical research or new information obtained for a specific reason. Data can also be collected from customers and site visitors or can be purchased from other organizations. The data a business collects from its customers is called first-party data. Data collected from a company (a competitor) that collected its own data is called second-party data. Finally, buying data from an enterprise that sells it is called third-party data.

The amount of data that businesses can obtain thanks to technology is impressive. By checking your analytics, a business organization can see its audience's demographics, interests, psychographics, consumer behaviors, predictive analytics, and more.

But in general, consumer data can be broken into four sections:

1. Personal data: Personally identifiable information such as gender and social security numbers. It can also include your IP address, web browser cookies, and device IDs (both on mobile and desktop devices).
2. Engagement data: How customers interact with a business's content. It includes the average order value, page likes, shares, and comments, how many people use your customer support system, etc.
3. Behavioral data: How much time customers spend browsing your content, mouse movement, purchase histories, and product usage information such as repeated actions.
4. Attitudinal data: Key metrics on purchase criteria, customer satisfaction, product desirability, opinions, branding, and sentiments.

All of this information can help a business organization to hyper-target its ads to get the best results and create content around what its audience engages with most. Netflix is a leading example of a use case of data analytics for marketing. They track their subscriber's search and watch data to know which movies to suggest. Smart suggestions like these keep subscribers' interest high, and in turn, they keep their memberships.

CHAPTER SIX

Consumer Protection Act, 2019

"*Learning Objectives*

- *Understand the applicability of the act*
- *Know the rights of the consumers*
- *Explain the definitions under the consumer protection act*
- *Know the Redressal Machinery under the Act*
- *Discuss the powers of the Dispute Redressal Agencies*

Lorose

Introduction

In business, consumers occupy a very important place. The consumer is the king of any business. The producers produce goods on the basis of the tastes, likings, preferences, etc. of the consumers. The consumer is the central point around which business activities revolve. Inspite of the great importance of consumers, they may be victims of immoral businessmen. An important aspect is that there is a lack of knowledge on the part of consumers and they are not organized as opposed to the sellers who are well-informed and organized. To protect consumers from unscrupulous businessmen and to provide an easy remedy for their complaints, the Consumer Protection Act was passed in the year 1986.

Before Consumer Protection Act, 1986 all the matters related to consumers are covered under MRTP Act 1969 (Monopolistic and Restrictive Trade Practices Act). The Monopolistic and Restrictive Trade Practices Legislation (MRTP) was implemented in 1969. This law was designed to ensure that the economic system's operation does not result in the concentration of economic power in the hands of a few. Which ensures that monopolies are controlled and that monopolistic and restrictive business practices are prohibited. MRTP Act basically deals with three distinctive topics i.e. Monopoly Trade practice, Restrictive trade practice, Unfair trade practice. A monopolistic trade practice involves the abuse of market power in the production and marketing of goods and services by excluding potential competitors, charging unreasonably high prices, preventing or restricting competition, limiting technological development, deteriorating product quality, and so on. Unfair business practice means a business practice that employs a dishonest or misleading practice to promote the sale, usage, or supply of products or services. But it was observed that only Unfair trade practice cases were very much registered under this MRTP Act. So to reduce the burden and maintain a proper consumer redressal mechanism this Consumer Protection Act,1986 was introduced. The new Consumer Protection Bill, 2019 replaces The Consumer Protection Act, 1986 ("Consumer Protection Act"), The Consumer Affairs, Food, and Public Distribution Minister, Ram Vilas Paswan, introduced the Consumer Protection Act, 2019 as a substitute for Copra 1986 on July 8, 2019, in the Lok Sabha. It was approved by the Lok Sabha on July 30, 2019, and the Rajya Sabha approved it on August 6, 2019.

Scope and Applicability of the Act

1. The act applies to all goods and services unless specifically exempted by the central government.
2. It covers all the sectors whether private, public, or corporative.
3. The provisions of the act are compensatory in nature.
4. It enshrines the following rights of consumers.
5. The act envisages the establishment of consumer protection councils at the
6. central and state levels, whose main objectives will be to promote and protect the rights of consumers.
7. The provisions of this act ate in addition to and not in derogation of the provisions of any other law for the time being in force.

Most common business malpractices

Consumer Protection Act provides better and all-around protection to consumers and effective safeguards against different types of exploitation such as defective goods, defective services,s and various unfair trade practices. It also makes provisions for simple and speedy and inexpensive machinery for the redressal of consumer grievances. Some of the most common business malpractices are -

- Sales of adulterated goods.
- Sales of suspecious goods.
- Sales of sub-standard goods.
- Sales of duplicate goods.
- Use of false weight and measures, underweight.
- Hoarding and black marketing of products lead to scarcity of goods or artificial raising of prices.
- Charging more than MRP.
- Supply of defective goods.
- Misleading advertisement.
- Supply of inferior service.

Definition of Consumer as per the Act

A consumer can be defined in terms of goods, and services, and in respect of both goods and services.

- As per section 2 (7) (i) consumer means any person who- buys any goods for a consideration which has been paid or promised or partly paid and partly promised, or under any system of deferred payment and includes any user of such goods other than the person who buys such goods for consideration paid or promised or partly paid or partly promised or under any system of deferred payment when such use is made with the approval of a such person.
- In general, we can say that a consumer is any person who buys goods or services in exchange for consideration and utilize such goods and services for personal use and not for the purpose of resale or commercial use.

- A consumer is a person who hires or avails of any services for a consideration that has been paid or promised or partly paid and partly promised, or under any system of deferred payment and includes any beneficiary of such services other than the person who hires or avails of the services for consideration paid or promised, or partly paid and partly promised, or under any system of deferred payment when such services are availed of with the approval of the first-mentioned person (but does not include a person who avails of such services of any commercial purpose).

Examples:

1. Mr. Saranjit purchased a car for his personal use. He is a consumer. But if he let out his car as a taxi he will not be regarded as a consumer.
2. An applicant for a ration card is not a consumer.

Who is "any person" as defined under the Consumer Protection Act, 2019?

As per section 2 (31) "person" includes

- An individual
- A firm whether registered or not.
- A Hindu undivided family.
- A cooperative society.
- An association of persons whether registered under the Societies Registration Act, 1860 (21 of 1860) or not.
- Any corporation, company, or body of individuals whether incorporated or not.
- Any artificial juridical person, not falling within any of the preceding sub-clauses.

What is a "Defect" as per the Act?

"Defect" means any fault, imperfection, or shortcoming in the quality, quantity, potency, purity, or standard which is required to be maintained by or under any law for the time being in force or under any contract, express or implied or as is claimed by the trader in any manner whatsoever in relation to any goods and the expression "defective" shall be construed accordingly.

What is a "Complaint" as per the Act?

"Complaint" means any allegation in writing made by a complainant that

1. An unfair trade practice or a restrictive trade practice has been adopted by any trader or service provider.
2. The goods bought by him or agreed to be bought by him suffer from one or more defects;
3. The services hired or availed of or agreed to be hired or availed of by him suffer from a deficiency in any respect.
4. Services that are hazardous or likely to be hazardous to the life and safety of the public when used, are being offered by the service provider which such a person could have known with due diligence to be injurious to life and safety.
5. he has suffered a loss due to an unfair contract entered into by him, with a view to obtaining any relief provided by or under this Act.

How to file a complaint?

Sec2 (c) Complaint means any allegation in writing made by a complainant. The complaint must cover the following points-

*   In the complaint, a consumer should mention the details of the problem. This can be exchange, replacement, or compensation for mental and physical torture. However, the declaration needs to be reasonable.
*   The relevant documents related to the complaint like bills, receipts, R/R, etc. must be attached to the complaint.
*   Acknowledgment is very important and should not be forgotten to receive by the complainant.
*   Complaints can be done in the form of a written application, via e-mail, fax, or any other media.
*   No need to hire a Lawer for the case.

What is a misleading advertisement?

Consumer Protection Act 2019 also covers the protection of customers from misleading advertisements. Manufacturers, advertising agencies, celebrity endorsers, and publishers can be made liable for misleading advertisements. It" can be defined in relation to any product or service, means an advertisement, which—

- Falsely describes such product or service; or
- Gives a false guarantee to, or is likely to mislead the consumers as to the nature, substance, quantity, or quality of such product or service; or
- Conveys an express or implied representation which, if made by the manufacturer or seller or service provider thereof, would constitute an unfair trade practice;
- Deliberately conceals important information

Right of a Consumer

The government of India provided the following rights to all consumers under the Consumer Protection Act:

1. Right to Safety
2. Right to information
3. Right to choice
4. Right to be heard
5. Right to seek redressal
6. Right-to-consumer education.

Right to Safety: According to this right the consumers have the right to be protected against the marketing of goods and services which are hazardous to life and property, this right is important for a safe and secure life. This right includes concern for consumers' long-term interests as well as for their present requirements. Sometimes manufacturing defects in pressure cookers, gas cylinders, and other electrical appliances may cause loss of life, health, and property of customers. This right to safety protects the consumer from the sale of such hazardous goods or services.

Right to information: According to this right the consumer has the right to get information about the quality, quantity, purity, standard, and price of goods or services so as to protect himself against abusive and unfair practices. The producer must supply all the relevant information at a suitable place.

Right to safety: According to this right every consumer has the right to choose the goods or services of his or her liking. The right to choose means an assurance of availability, ability, and access to a variety of products and services at competitive prices and competitive price means just or fair price. The producer or supplier or retailer should not force the customer to buy a particular brand only. Consumers should be free to choose the most suitable product from their point of view.

Right to be heard: According to this right, the consumer has the right to represent him or to be heard or

right to advocate his interest. In case a consumer has been exploited or has any complaint against the product or service then he has the right to be heard and be assured that his/ her interest would receive due consideration. This right includes the right to representation in the government and in other policy-making bodies. Under this right, the companies must have complaint cells to attend to the complaints of customers.

Right to seek redressal: The consumer has the right to get compensation or seek redressal against unfair

trade practices or any other exploitation. This right assures justice to consumers against exploitation. The right to redressal includes compensation in the form of money or replacement of goods or repair of defects in the goods as per the satisfaction of the consumer. Various redressal forums are set up by the government at the district level, national level, and state levels.

Right to consumer education: It is the right of consumers to acquire the knowledge and skills to be informed to customers. It is easier for literate consumers to know their rights and take action but this right assures that illiterate consumers can seek information about the existing acts and agencies set up for their protection. The government of India has included consumer education in the school curriculum and in various university courses. The government is also making use of media to make consumers aware of

their rights and make wise use of their money.

Redressal agencies under Consumer Protection Act 2015

According to Section 9, there shall be established for the purposes of this Act, the following agencies, namely:

1. A District Consumer Grievance Redressal Commission is to be known as the "District Commission" and is established by the State Government in each district of the State by notification: Provided that the State Government may, if it deems fit, establish more than one District Commission in a district.
2. A State Consumer Disputes Redressal Commission to be known as the "State Commission" is established by the State Government in the State by notification
3. A National Consumer Disputes Redressal Commission to be known as the "National Commission" was established by the Central Government by notification.

District forum: Subject to the other provisions of this Act, the District Commission shall have jurisdiction to entertain complaints where the billed value of the goods or services claimed does not exceed rupees of One Cr, or up to thrice the limits of such value as may be prescribed. The District Commission shall ordinarily function in the district headquarters and may perform its functions at such other place in the district, as the State Government may, in consultation with the State Commission, notify in the Official
Gazette from time to time. Each District Commission shall consist of the following-

- A person who is, or has been, or is qualified to be a District Judge or an officer not below the rank of a District Magistrate in the State or equivalent, who shall be its President.
- There must be a minimum of two members in the district consumer forum, at least one of whom shall be a woman, The eligibility criteria for members are - Who shall be not less than thirty-five years of age; Must possess a bachelor's degree from a recognized university; and must be a person of ability, integrity, and standing, and have adequate
- The person must have adequate knowledge and experience in the same field of at least a minimum of 10 years of experience in dealing with

problems related to law, economics, accounts, industry, public affairs, and administration.

State Commission: Each State Commission shall consist of—

1. A person who is or has been a Judge of a High Court, appointed by the State Government, who shall be its President: Provided that no appointment under this clause shall be made except after consultation with the Chief Justice of the High Court;
2. In a state commission, there must be a minimum of four members and one of whom shall be a woman, who shall have the following qualifications, namely-

- be not less than forty years of age;
- Possess a bachelor's degree from a recognized university;
- Be persons of ability, integrity, and standing, and have adequate knowledge and experience of at least ten years in dealing with problems relating to economics, law, commerce, accountancy, industry, consumer affairs, or administration.

Jurisdiction of the State commission:
1. Subject to the other provisions of this Act, the State Commission shall have jurisdiction to entertain-

- Complaints where the billed value of the goods or services, exceeds rupees fifty lakhs but does not exceed rupees ten crores or up to thrice the limits of the said value as may be prescribed; and
- appeals against the orders of any District Commission within the State; and
- To call for the records and pass appropriate orders in any consumer dispute which is pending before or has been decided by any District Commission within the State, where it appears to the State Commission that such District Commission has exercised a jurisdiction not vested in it by law, or has failed to exercise a jurisdiction so vested or has acted in exercise of its jurisdiction illegally or with material irregularity.

2. A complaint shall be instituted in a State Commission within the limits of whose jurisdiction,-

- The opposite party or each of the opposite parties, where there is more than one, at the time of the institution of the complaint, actually and voluntarily resides or carries on business or has a branch office or personally works for gain; or
- Any of the opposite parties, where there are more than one, at the time of the institution of the complaint, actually and voluntarily resides, or carries on business or has a branch office or personally works for gain, provided that in such case the permission of the State Commission is given; or
- The cause of action, wholly or in part, arises;
- The complainant resides or personally works for gain.

Officers and employees of the State Commission:

1. The State Government shall determine the nature and categories of the officers and other employees required to assist the State Commission in the discharge of its functions and provide the Commission with such officers and other employees as it may think fit.
2. The officers and other employees of the State Commission shall discharge their functions under the general superintendence of the President.
3. The salaries and allowances payable to and the other terms and conditions of service of, the officers and other employees of the State Commission shall be such as may be prescribed by the State Government.

Appeal to the national commission:

1. Any person aggrieved by an order made by the State Commission in the exercise of its powers conferred by sub-clause (i) of clause (a) of sub-section (1) of section 40 may prefer an appeal against such an order to the National Commission within a period of thirty days from the date of the order in such form and manner as may be prescribed:

- Provided that the National Commission shall not entertain the appeal after the expiry of the said period of thirty days unless it is satisfied that there was sufficient cause for not filing it within that period.
- Provided further that no appeal by a person, who is required to pay any amount in terms of an order of the State Commission, shall be

entertained by the National Commission unless the appellant has deposited in a prescribed manner fifty percent of that amount.

2. Save as otherwise expressly provided under this Act or by any other law for the time being in force, an appeal shall lie to the National Commission from any order passed in appeal by any State Commission, if the National Commission is satisfied that the case involves a substantial question of law.

3. An appeal may lie to the National Commission under this section from an order passed ex parte by the State Commission.

4. In an appeal under this section, the memorandum of appeal shall precisely state the substantial question of law involved in the appeal.

5. Where the National Commission is satisfied that a substantial question of law is involved in any case, it shall formulate that question.

6. The appeal shall be heard on the question so formulated and the respondent shall, after hearing the appeal, be allowed to argue that the case does not involve such questions.

Provided that nothing in this sub-section shall be deemed to take away or abridge the power of the National Commission to hear, for reasons to be recorded in writing, the appeal on any other substantial question of law, if it is satisfied that the case involves a such question of law.

Jurisdiction of the National Commission :

A. Subject to the other provisions of this Act, the National Commission shall have jurisdiction to entertain-

1. complaints, where the billed value of the goods or services claimed, exceeds rupees ten crores or up to thrice the limits of the said value as may be prescribed; and
2. Appeals against the orders of any State Commission; and
3. To call for the records and pass appropriate orders in any consumer dispute which is pending before or has been decided by any State Commission where it appears to the National Commission that such State Commission has exercised a jurisdiction not vested in it by law, or has failed to exercise a jurisdiction so vested, or has acted in the exercise of its jurisdiction illegally or with material irregularity.

B . The jurisdiction, powers, and Central Authority of the National Commission may be exercised by Benches thereof-

- A Bench may be constituted by the President with one or more members as the President deems fit:
- Provided that the senior most member of the Bench shall preside over the Bench.
- If the Members of a Bench differ in opinion on any point, the points shall be decided according to the opinion of the majority, if there is a majority, but if the members are equally divided, they shall state the point or points on which they differ, and make a reference to the President who shall either hear the point or points himself or refer the case for hearing on such point or points by one or more of the other Members and such point or points shall be decided according to the opinion of the majority of the Members who have heard the case, including those who first heard it: Provided that the President or the Members, as the case may be, shall give his or their opinion on the point or points referred to him or them within a period of two months from the date of such reference.

Reliefs are provided by Consumer Commissions:

The complaint must be submitted within two years of the occurrence of the cause of action. This would imply a two-year period beginning on the day the service or product defect first occurred or was discovered. This is also known as the deadline for submitting a complaint. Following reliefs may be provided by the Consumer redressal agencies-

- Removal of defects from the goods;
- Replacement of the goods; iii. Refund of the price paid;
- Removal of defects or deficiencies in the services;
- Award of compensation for the loss or injury suffered;
- Discontinue and not repeat unfair trade practice or restrictive trade practices;
- To withdraw hazardous goods from being offered for sale;
- To cease the manufacture of hazardous goods and desist from offering services that are hazardous in nature;
- If the loss or injury has been suffered by a large number of consumers who are not identifiable conveniently, to pay such sum (not less than 25% of the value of such defective goods or services provided) which shall be determined by the Commission;
- To issue corrective advertisements to neutralize the effect of misleading advertisements;

- To provide adequate costs to parties.

Any consumer who is aggrieved by the order of a commission can prefer an appeal to the higher commission within a period of thirty days from the date of the order. The appeal can be preferred against the order of the District Commission before the State Commission within 30 days, against the order of the State Commission before the National Commission within 30 days, and against the order of the National Commission before the Supreme Court within 45 days.

Fee for filing a complaint with the Commission:

Every complaint must be preceded by a fee, as detailed in the table below, payable at the location where the District Commission, State Commission, or National Commission is located, in the form of a crossed Demand Draft drawn on a nationalized bank or through a crossed Indian Postal Order in favor of the President of the District Commission, the Registrar of the State Commission, or the Registrar of the National Commission.

Sl.No	Value of Goods or Service paid as Consideration	Court Fee
	District Commission	
1	Upto 5 Lakh	Nil
2	Above 5 Lakh – Upto 10 Lakh	Rs 200
3	Above 10 lakh – Upto 20 Lakh	Rs 400
4	Above 20 Lakh – Upto 50 Lakh	Rs 1000
5	Above 50 Lakh – Upto 1 Crore	Rs 2000
	State Commission	
6	Above 1 Crore – Upto 2 Crore	Rs 2500
7	Above 2 Crore – Upto 4 Crore	Rs 3000
8	Above 4 Crore – Upto 6 Crore	Rs 4000
9	Above 6 Crore – Upto 8 Crore	Rs 5000
10	Above 8 Crore – Upto 10 Crore	Rs 6000
	National Commission	
11	Above 10 Crore	Rs 7500

Exhibit 6.1 : Fee for filling a complanit with the Commission

CHAPTER SEVEN

Question Bank

1. What do you mean by "Consumer Behaviour"?
2. What are the determinants of Consumer behaviour?
3. What do you mean by consumer black box?
4. What are emotional buying motives?
5. What is Pactronage buying motive?
6. What do you mean by "Opinion leader" and "Opinion Seeker"?
7. What do you understand by consumer learning?
8. Write about the various micro factors affecting consumer behaviour.
9. Discuss how consumer values and lifestyle affect the buying behaviour of an individual.
10. Write down the difference between Consumer buying Behaviour vs Industrial buying behaviour.
11. How do personality and self-concept affect consumer behaviour?
12. Discuss how the study of consumer behaviour can help in appropriate market segmentation and product positioning.
13. "Consumer behaviour is a field of study that examines external influences on consumption decisions" Justify the statement.
14. How do personality and self-concept affect consumer behaviour?
15. Identify the physiological factors that may affect consumer behaviour.
16. "Consumer Behaviour incorporates several Major Aspects of Disciplines such as Sociology, Psychology, Anthropology, and Economics." Elucidate.
17. . Give an account of the Various Methods of 'Consumer Research'.
18. What do you mean by Buying motive? Explain various types of buying motives. What is the importance of motivation in consumer behaviour?
19. What is social comparison theory? How does it relate to status consumption? What are the methods of social class measurement? Talk

about one of them in brief.

20. What are the three levels of consumer decision-making? Briefly define each. Explain the economic consumer model. Why is this model considered to be unrealistic in nature?

21. What do you mean by Cognitive dissonance? Write various methods to deal with cognitive dissonance.

22. What do you know about "Consumer Involvement"?

23. Explain the difference between culture and sub-culture. What is the role of culture in consumer behaviour?

24. What are reference groups?

25. Discuss the impact of social class on buying behaviour.

26. What is the first step of an information search?

27. What do you mean by consumer satisfaction?

28. What are the various phases of consumer satisfaction?

29. Explain the various phases of the consumer decision-making process.

30. What do you mean by "Evoked set", "Inept set", and "Inert set"?

31. What do you mean by post-purchase behaviour?

32. Explain the consumer's postpurchase evaluation process.

33. How a consumer can identify his needs? What are the stimuli associated with this process of consumer buying behaviour?

34. Explain the term " Diffusion of innovation"

35. Describe the benefits of the Consumer Protection Act 2019 to the Indian consumer.

36. How can knowledge of personality be used to develop a marketing strategy?

37. What is Culture? Explain Cross Cultural understanding of Consumer Behaviour.

38. What is Learning? Explain the importance of Learning in understanding Consumer Behaviour.

39. What is Consumer Dispute? Explain the various Consumer Disputes Redressal Forums.

40. What is Market Segmentation? Explain the relationship between Demographic Characteristics and Market Segmentation.

41. What do you mean by Ideal level of service expectation?

42. Write a brief note on Consumer behaviour in the Indian context.

43. Explain the Habitual Buying Process Model of Engel Kollat and Blackwell.

44. Analyze the Changing Role of Families on consumer behaviour.

45. " An opinion leader has different characteristics than others" Justify the statement.

46. How to Distinguish between customer and consumer with the help of suitable examples. Discuss the importance of consumer research in the discipline of consumer behaviour consumer lifestyles play an important role in their buying behaviour?

47. What is the difference between selective attention and perceptual defence? What are the basic principles of Perception?

48. Discuss the relevance of the Engel-Kollat model in the study of consumer behaviour. actual organization.

49. Discuss the post-purchase behaviour of Consumers.

50. Discuss the influence of communication on consumer behaviour.

51. What do you mean by the pre-purchase behaviour of consumers?

52. Explain the basic elements of diffusion of innovation.

53. Explain the various dimensions of Consumer behaviour.

54. Discuss the interrelationships among customer expectations and satisfaction, perceived value, and customer retention. Why is customer retention essential?

55. Identify the sources of influence on attitude formation. Outline and explain the five strategies for changing consumer attitudes.

56. Why self-image is important in consumer behaviour?

57. Explain the role of value and attitude in purchasing decisions.

58. Explain the behavioral theories of learning. Highlight their applications in the field of consumer behavior.

59. Explain classical conditioning theory of learning. How this theory can be used in buying behaviour. Explain with suitable example.

60. Write a note on Data drieve disicion making.